THE NAMES OF THE SUBSCRIBERS.

A
HIS Grace the Duke of Argyle
John Aiſlabie, *Eſq*;

B
Earl of Buchan
Alexander Brodie, of Brodie, *Lord* Lyon
Sir William Billers
John Banks, *Eſq*;
Thomas Beuois, *Eſq*;
George Beale, *Eſq*;
Counteſs of Berkſhire
Mrs. Urſula Baker
Mrs Bowes

C
Sir James Campbell *Bar.*
Sir Nath. Curzon, *Bart.*
Sir Robert Saliſbury Cotton, *Bart.*
William Crow, *Eſq*;
Peter Cary, *Eſq*;
Daniel Campbell, *Eſq*;
Thomas Clark, *Eſq*;
William Conolly, *Eſq*; 2 *Books.*
John Campbell, *Eſq*;
Colonel Carpenter
Dr. Campbell
Lady Frances Clifton
Lady Coningſby
Mrs. M. Campbell
Mrs. Cooper

D
Sir J. Dalrimple, *Bart.*
Right Honourable George Doddington, *Eſq:*
Stephen D'Aubus, *Eſq*;
——Dumer, *Eſq*;
Mr. Dalzel
Lady Dudley

E
Sir Richard Ellys, *Bart.*
Rich. Edgcombe, *Eſq*;
Mr. Eadnell
Mrs. Edwards

F Henry

The Subscribers Names.

F
Henry Furness, *Esq*;
Mrs. Folkingham

G
Earl of Gainsborough
Lord Gower
Sir Arch. Grant, *Bart.*
Sir R. Grosvenor, *Bart.*
Rob. Grosvenor, *Esq*;
Barn. Goldsworthy, *Esq*;
General Gledhil
Captain Gumeldon
Mr. Gashry

H
James Hall, *Esq*;
Aaron Hill, *Esq*;
John Hilton, *Esq*,
William Harbert, *Esq*;
Lady Jane Holt
Mrs. Hart

L
Sir Thomas Lowther
Thomas Lunn, *Esq*;

M
Earl of Marchmont
Lord Viscount Micklethwait
Lord Muskerry
John Manby, *Esq*;
Mr. Thomas Manlove
Lady Doddington Montague
Mrs. Sarah Mellis
Mrs. Kath. Matthews

N
Earl of Northampton
Sir Michael Newton

O
Her Grace the Dutchess of Ormonde
John Opie, *Esq*; 2 Books.

P
Sir Herbert Perrot Packington, *Bart.*
Walter Plumer, *Esq*;
John Peacock, *Esq*;

R
John Raper, *Esq*;
William Raper, *Esq*;

S
Earl of Stair
Sir John Shaw, *Bart.*
Colonel James Scot
The Rev. John Sandford, *Curate of* Hornsey.
Mrs. Frances Skelton
Mrs. Scot

T
Earl of Thanet
Jacob Trible, *Esq*;

V
Gerard Vanneck, *Esq*;
Joshua Vanneck, *Esq*;

W
Mrs. Webster
Mrs. Ann Ward

SECRET MEMOIRS

Of the late

Mr. *Duncan Campbel*,

The Famous

Deaf and Dumb Gentleman.

WRITTEN

By HIMSELF, who ordered they should be publish'd after his Decease.

To which is added,
An APPENDIX, by Way of VINDICATION of Mr. DUNCAN CAMPBEL, against that groundless Aspersion cast upon him, *That he but pretended to be Deaf and Dumb.*

The Lucky have whole Days, which still they chuse,
Th' Unlucky have but Hours, and those they lose.
DRYDEN.

THE CONTENTS.

THE *Introduction* — Page 1
Chap. I. *Of Fortune-telling in General* — 5
Chap. II. *On my Enemies* — 12
Chap. III. *Some convincing Proofs that I always preferred the Interest of my Consulters to my Own* — 20
Chap. IV. *On Witchcraft* — 37
Chap. V. *On the various Deceptions endeavoured to be put on Me* — 47
Chap. VI. *On Omens: Which are to be depended on, and which not.* — 60
Chap. VII. *On Predestination* — 77
Chap. VIII. *On the Power of Sympathy* — 84
Chap. IX. *On the Difference between Natural and Diabolical Magic* — 97
Chap. X. *On Apparitions* — 103
Chap. XI. *On the Genii* — 118
Chap. XII. *On the Second-Sight* — 129
Chap. XIII. *On the Virtues of the Loadstone, and some other choice Curiosities in Nature* — 133
Chap. XIV. *Containing some Examples of the Unreasonable Things frequently required of me* — 142
Chap. XV. *A Remarkable Instance of Ingratitude* — 158
The Friendly Dæmon; or, the Generous Apparition — 166
Original

CONTENTS.

Original LETTERS sent to Mr. CAMPBEL by his Consulters.

Let. I. *From a Person under great Misfortunes* 196
Let. II. *From a Gentleman in the Country* 198
Let. III. *From a Lady, who, from the Depth of Misery, was suddenly raised to Happiness* 200
Let. IV. *From an old Correspondent.* 201
Let. V. *From a Jew residing at* Constantinople 204
Let. VI. *From a Lady of Distinction* 205
Let. VII. *From the same* 207
Let. VIII. *From a young Lady very much in Love* 208
Let. IX. *From a Politician* 209
Let. X. *From a young Nobleman* 211
Let. XI. *From a Gentleman to whom Mr.* Campbel *had lent the Book of his Life, and Spy on the Conjurer* 212
Let. XII. *From a new-married Lady* 213
Let. XIII. *From an Adept* 215
Let. XIV. *From a young Gentleman at* Cambridge 217
Let. XV. *From a Gentleman of the Town* 218
Let. XVI. *From a Gentleman at* Bombay 220
Let. XVII. *From an old Lady married to a young Man* 221
Let. XVIII. *From a Person of Quality* 222
An Appendix, by Way of Vindication of Mr. Duncan Campbel, *against that groundless Aspersion, cast upon him, that he but pretended to be Deaf and Dumb* 227

THE

THE INTRODUCTION.

S no Person who has made any Noise in the World, either for good or bad Qualifications, can die without exciting a Curiosity in the Publick to know something more after his Death, than could possibly be learned while he lived, I doubt not, but as soon as I shall *cease to be*, several Pens will be employed in relating *what I have been*; and therefore think it more proper to write my own Life (with which I am certainly best acquainted) than to leave it to the Mercy of some Hackney Scribler or other, who, perhaps, is altogether ignorant of every Thing concerning me but my Name and Profession, yet will pretend to know more of me than ever God Almighty did.

To comply with the Taste of the Times then, I shall leave something to Posterity, tho' not to please the Rabble, nor the Learned, if ill-natured: I only aim to gratify such after my Death, as were pleased with me when living. Perhaps the World will call 'em Fools, but every one knows what Answer those People deserve who go with the Million: I shall only say, *Had only the Illiterate been satisfied with my Predictions, I should long since have fallen into the Fate of common Fortune-tellers, made a Flash at first like lighted Gunpowder, then lost all my Force in Smoak, and have been no more remembered; whereas for thirty eight Years I have stood my Ground in Defiance of all my Adversaries, though I have had many and powerful ones.* Nor was it those of the fair Sex alone who gave Credit to my Art; the most Wise, Grave and Judicious of the other have thought it worthy their Regard: Some even of the Royal Cabinet have proved the *Dumb Man* no Imposture, and after consulting me, would have pay'd me greater Adorations than became a Mortal to receive.

I KNOW there is nothing more generally exploded by those who would be thought wise Men, than the whole Mystery of foretelling Events; but as I doubt not, but this little Treatise will fall into the Hands of Numbers who have profited by my Skill, I shall leave it to them to speak in its Vindication, and I appeal to all

who,

who, on my Subject, have confulted me, and not only to them, but to that fuperior Power, that Being of Beings, before whom we muft all be judged, and to whom I fhall anfwer, before ever this fees the Light, if I ever gave Advice to the Detriment of any Perfon, or did not, to the utmoft of my Power, endeavour to prevent the Mifchiefs I forefaw would threaten them: But 'tis enough for People of flender Capacities to exclaim againft what they cannot comprehend. Not that I fay all are Weak who reject my Predictions; no, I know many great, and truly wife Men in other Things, who will not fuffer themfelves to give Credit to any thing I fhould fay, merely becaufe they would not feem to give into that Foible of being Superftitious; but I would fain afk thofe Gentlemen, if, on ftrict Examination of themfelves, they have not fome darling Failing of, perhaps, worfe Confequence to indulge. There is no Perfection on this fide Heaven, and I folemnly aver, that I never found greater Follies in the moft ftupid and ignorant of my Confulters, than I have in fome of thofe who were regarded by the World as Prodigies of Wit and Learning. But this is not my Bufinefs; all that I pretend to by this little Account of myfelf is, to prevent thofe I have a Value for from being impofed on by a fpurious Relation, and to give fome Reafons in Defence of my Art after my Death, which would not fo readily obtain Credit while I live: 'Tis a known Truth, that whatever Vices Youth, Inadvertency, Temptation, and the Custom of the Times may have led me into, I was never abandoned in my Principles, but had always a just Sense of Right and Wrong, accompanied with a Hope of future Happiness, and Terror for its Punishments; none therefore can be so Barbarous as to imagine I would wish to quit the World with a Fallacy, as I must do if I wrote any Thing here in Injury to Truth, because, though at this Time I am in a tollerable State of Health, whenever I shall be called hence, this is my last Will and Testament to the Publick, and ought to be depended on as much as the last Words of a dying Man.

M E-

MEMOIRS

Of the late Famous

Mr. *Duncan Campbel.*

✱✱✱✱✱✱✱✱✱✱✱✱✱✱✱✱✱✱✱✱

CHAP. I.

Of FORTUNETELLING *in General.*

THE Particulars of my Birth and Parentage, with my firſt Inſpiration of ſeeing Things to come, having been ſufficiently treated on, in a Book entitled, *The Life of Mr.* Duncan Campbel, would be needleſs for me to repeat what is there ſo fully related. I ſhall therefore begin with my coming to *London*: And, I hope, none will accuſe me of Profaneneſs, when I compare myſelf in this Point to *Joſeph*, who, by a Dream, was conducted to *Egypt*, ſince it was the ſame God, who, by his miniſtring Angel, took the ſame Means to ſend me to this great City, where I have acquired both a Livelihood and Reputation, as much

much beyond my Hope or Expectation as his were.

I very well know, that from my Birth I have had the conſtant Attendance of both a good and bad Angel: I am confident of it, and have ſuch undeniable Proofs, that the Being of a Sun, Moon, or Stars is not more certain to me, nor do I aſcribe any thing extraordinary to myſelf in this: It is my Opinion, that great Numbers of People, eſpecially in the firſt Ages of the World, have been thus attended, and even in theſe latter Times, many are hindred only by their own Unbelief, from receiving Marks as evident and demonſtrative as I have done of this peculiar Proof, how greatly we Mortals are the Care of Providence. If I underſtand the Story of *Balaam* and his Aſs right, he was one of thoſe I have been ſpeaking of. Hiſtory abounds with Examples of Men who have ſeen and converſed with theſe ſupernatural Intelligencies, and, I believe it no leſs true, that many of the *Jews* enjoy that Privilege to this Day. I have been honoured with the Acquaintance of ſome of their *Rabbies*, and could not avoid feeling for them a ſecret Veneration, which not all my Deteſtation of the Enemies of *Chriſtianity* could extinguiſh: Nay, I could not avoid, in ſpite of their preſent Unbelief, aſſuring myſelf, that ſome among them were highly favoured by Heaven. 'Tis certain, I knew one who poſſeſſed Secrets which raiſed him to the utmoſt Pitch of Knowledge

Hu-

Humanity can arrive to: He obliged me with one by which I have got some *hundred* Pounds, and which there are People would have made *Thousands* of, and is, indeed, of an inestimable Value; this is the Art of making *Talismans*. As the Planets have undoubtedly an Influence over all Things in this lower World, so they themselves are also governed by Numbers; and Numbers, if rightly understood, have a Power in them beyond what Humanity is capable of conceiving. The true Use of them is certainly the Tree of Knowledge; it is in them the whole Art of Magick consists, and by them a Mortal might not only be enabled to judge of all Things in Nature, but also of what is truly Good or truly Evil, and to excel in the most sublime and supernatural Acts of either, even to the bringing Angels down to converse with him on Earth, or raising the Infernal Spirits to the Light of the Sun. *Talismans*, therefore, being entirely directed by Numbers and Proportion, and made at a Time when the beneficent Planets have Influence, ought not to be condemned by Persons the most averse to Superstition; and it would be as stupid to deny their Force, as it would be to refuse the Sun the Honour of warming us, or the Moon her Influence over the Tides. Reason then teaches us to value so noble a Science, nor does Piety in the least oppose it. The ancient Patriarchs, who undoubtedly, did every Thing by Inspiration, were the first Inventors of them; and *Moses* afterwards wore a *Talisman*, to which

which, as to a second Cause under Heaven, we are to ascribe the Wonders he performed. Since him the most eminent in all Ages made Use of them, and the wise Men among the *Persians* and *Chaldeans* had them in the extreamest Veneration; and if it were put to the Test, I believe it might be proved, that some late great Generals and Statesmen undertook no important Affair without having a *Talisman* about them.

It is but to few of my Consulters I have imparted this Secret, knowing it in the Power of my own Art, to answer (except some very extraordinary Accident intervened) the several Queries they demanded; not but I have now by me a good Number of those wonderful Parchments, and hope to make more, but I shall defer the general Use of them till after my Death, not doubting but they will be a Legacy of Value to my Family when I am gone, if I should, by long Sickness, or other Misfortunes, be deprived of leaving any thing beside. God only knows the Time and Pains they cost me in making, and how many Hours I have borrowed from my Sleep to watch the happy Constellation, under which alone they can be rendered useful. The Knowledge, how excellent in numberless Cases these *Talismans* are, assures me I shall live many Ages hence in their mysterious Virtues, and that whoever wears them, will acknowledge *Duncan Campbel* no less Studious for the Good of the World

World at his going out of it, than he always proved himself while he lived in it.

HERE I cannot omit reminding all such who depended on my Judgment, that there is nothing in what bears the Name of *Palmiſtry*: I have had a thouſand fine Hands held out to me in my Time, with the moſt earneſt Entreaty, that I would examine the Lines; and if I could have entertained the leaſt Thought of abuſing thoſe who put Confidence in me, I might eaſily have done it, by pretending to this Art; but I ſhould have been aſhamed to have been guilty of ſuch an Impoſition, nor could I have anſwered it to my Conſcience; and I am ſurprized to find ſo many, and ſome of them Men of Learning too, could have ſpent their Time ſo ill, as to write ſuch great Treatiſes of what has nothing of Reality in it: The Hands and Feet, though full of Lines, and ſo different, that, perhaps, there are not two in the World alike, and very few that have the leaſt Reſemblance of each other, have yet nothing in them prognoſticating either Good or Evil. *Phiſiognomy*, alſo, according to the common Rules ſet down for it, is as deluſive: Features are not the Marks of Fate; a Man may be full as Unfortunate with a high Forehead and ſmooth Brow, as he that has a very low one and full of Wrincles; nor is the Largeneſs of the Noſtrils, or Smallneſs of the Ears, always an Argument of Wit and Ingenuity: Much, indeed, is to be gathered from the Face, and

Neck

Neck, and much more from the Air and Mein; but then there are no Directions to be given for the Attainment of this Knowledge, nor is it to be learned, but muſt come by that Inſtinct, Inſpiration, or Divination, vulgarly called *Second Sight*.

I KNOW I ſhall be curs'd in my Grave by all the Calculators of Nativities, and Reſolvers of Hororary Queſtions, when I acquaint the World that it cannot ſuffer a greater Impoſition than what is made Uſe of by the Pretenders to this Science: I ſay the *Pretenders*, becauſe I have the utmoſt Eſteem for thoſe Gentlemen who are really Proficients in Aſtrology. Nothing is more certain, than that the Planets have an Influence not only on the Diſpoſitions and Humours of the Perſons born under them, but likewiſe over the Events that ſhall befal them; but if thoſe Perſons who come to conſult ſuch as commonly make a Practice of this Art, would conſider how vaſtly difficult it is to be attained, they would never imagine it could be comprehended by ſuch illiterate Wretches; ſome of whom are ſcarcely acquainted with their Mother Tongue. I was never in a greater Paſſion in my Life, than when one Day a Lady came to me, and having wrote her Buſineſs, added at the Bottom of the Paper, *That I had calculated her Mother's Nativity*. At firſt I thought ſhe had miſtook me for ſome other, but on recollecting myſelf, perceived how ſhe had fallen into this Error. To oblige

oblige several of my fair Consulters, I have frequently made up Paper in the Form of a Book, and alotting to each Leaf a Year, set down those remarkable Events which come within the Compass of my Art to discover. On one perhaps there might be the Figure of a Coffin, denoting the Death of some Friend or Relation; on another a Coronet, signifying Affairs with some of the Nobility; and various others Hierogliphicks, betokening the different Incidents in her Life: These the young Lady, doubtless, took either for Planets, or the Signs of the *Zodiack*, and me for an Astrologer; but I soon undeceived her, and told her, *My Talent lay another Way, and that I never practised that Science, nor indeed had sufficient Understanding in it to calculate a Nativity.* I wish all who are applied to as such, and know as little, or probably less than I do of it, would deal with the same Ingenuity, and not deceive their Clients by a few hard Words picked out of the Almanack, and irregular Scratches with the Pen, which they pass on the Credulous and Ignorant for the Twelve Houses, and Degrees of Constellation. As for the new-fashion'd Way of discovering future Events by Tea or Coffee-Grounds, I think it would be lost Time to make any Disertation; they are Amusements which I have often laughed at myself, and to divert the Company have thrown a Cup in my Turn; but I would not judge so ill of the World, as to imagine any body comes to consult these People with a serious

ous Inclination to believe a Word they say. If there be any such, I pity them, but look on them as Persons too far gone in Folly, for any thing either I, or a wiser Man can argue to reclaim.

CHAP. II.

On my Enemies.

AD I met with any Portion of that Candour and Sincertiy from my Consulters and Acquaintance, as I always treated them with, I had not lived to the Age of Fifty, without being possessed of some little Fortune to comfort my Decline; and, whenever I shall be removed to a better World, where all Cares cease, to have left for my Family's Support. I was once in a fair Way of being a great Court Favourite, and would not have given a Shilling to any Man to have insured me a handsome Pension. Her late Majesty Queen *Anne* was no Stranger to my Scrawls, and testified the Satisfaction I had given her, in a most beneficent Manner, by Mr. *Geeky*, her Majesty's Occulist at that Time. One Thing in particular that I wrote, she put among her Rarities, and told the Ladies
about

about her, *That it very well deserved that Place.* But just in this Crisis, my ill Angel got the Better of my good One, and deprived me of any further Marks of Royal Favour: My Lady F―――― having taken a sudden Picque against me, represented me to her Majesty as a Man of ill Principles and dangerous: Her Assertion was afterwards backed by my Lady *M*――――, who added, *That she had seen several very ill-looked Men in my House*; but I take God to be my Witness, her Ladyship never entered my Doors but twice, and that what she alledged was so far from the Truth, that not a living Soul, either of those Times, was under my Roof, but her Ladyship, my Wife, two Children, and a Servant Maid. These Ladies, only because I could not do what is beyond the Power of all Human Art, became my inveterate Enemies, and scrupled not to say all that the most witty Malice could invent against me; and so prevalent is Ill-Nature, in the greatest Part of the World, that I have known twenty or thirty beat out of their Reason by the Disappointment of one, and sometimes a pretended one too. Some who never saw my Face have been my greatest Aspersors, out of the most unaccountable Principle that can be imagined; it being impossible I could disoblige, in any Respect, Persons whom I did not so much as know by Character: But I was once in such a Vogue, that not to have been with me, was to have been out of the Fashion; and it was then as strange a

Thing

Thing not to have confulted the *Deaf and Dumb Conjurer*, as it is now not to have feen the *Beggars Opera* half a dozen Times, or to admire *Polly Peachum*. The Mode will ftill prevail; and new Things, of what Kind foever, will pleafe for a while. But I fwerve from my Purpofe: I fay I was once fo celebrated a Perfon, that thofe People, who wanted either Time or Money to confult me, were afhamed to own their Omiffion, and would be talking of me to convince their Acquaintance they were as much in the Fafhion as themfelves; fo that I impute great Part of the ridiculous Stories raifed on me, to be owing rather to Vanity than Malice. Bullies would fay, *They had beat me*; Whores, *That I had attempted their Virtue*; and Numbers to teftify the great Opinion I had of their Sagacity and Wifdom, would fwear, *I talked to them, and made ufe of converfing with my Pen, only in fuch Company as could not keep a Secret*. 'Tis certain, that becaufe I have fometimes difcovered the Means of retrieving loft Goods; every Servant Maid that had miffed a Silver Spoon, would come immediately to me for Directions where to find it, and if I refufed to oblige her, go away fpitting her Spite againft me to as many as fhe met. But in fuch Things I fhare the Fate of the greateft of Men in the Kingdom: The Treafury of the Nation would be but a Mite to fupply the Wants of all who are ready to become Petitioners; yet, tho' they fhould receive *Ninety nine* out of the *Hundred*, they would exclaim

againft

against the Avarice and Corruption of the Dispensors. The Ingratitude of the World is such, that even between Friend and Friend, though the one sacrifices three Parts of his Fortune to the other, yet shall he not be satisfied, and on Denial of the Fourth, repay all former Obligations with Calumny and Detraction. How often this has been my Case, God and my poor Family knows; but I have learnt to forgive, and hope the Injuries done to me and mine, will never rise against the Authors. I confess I have been too much a Libertine, and have thought Drinking, Fighting, running away with Men's Wives and Daughters, Gentlemen-like Qualifications, but these Exploits were in my younger Years, and greatly owing to the Company I then kept.

Of late, hard Study, and a constant Application to my Business, has brought Fits upon me, which some barbarous Wretches have given out were counterfeited: I would fain know for what Reason I should counterfeit a Condition so truly deplorable? I stood not at the Corner of a Street to move Compassion, and excite the Charity of those that passed; I was no Gainer, but a great Loser by this Misfortune: Few knew me without knowing I have been at more Expence than I was well able to sustain in Hope of Cure, and have frequently been obliged to turn away my best Customers. When I have been, to all Appearance, in the best Stare of Health that Ladies could

could be wished, and have had three or four fine Ladies with me, a Flirt of a Fan has made me suddenly drop down in the most terrible Convulsions, and rendered me wholly incapable of answering any Questions that Day. Would any Man chuse to distort his Face, and decay his Spirits with a forced Agony were he to lose nothing by it? But I am not only a Sufferer in my Constitution, by these cruel Enemies of Nature, but likewise in my Livelihood. As I have seldom any Warning of their coming upon me, it is the more frightful to myself, and every-body in the Room. At my Recovery, it adds to my Confusion to reflect how trifling a Thing has sometimes occasioned my Disorder, such as a Nurse dancing an Infant too quick in her Arms, my own Children running hastily cross the Room, the Sight of a Mouse, or, as I said before, the Flirt of a Fan: I have made use of my utmost Efforts to overcome this Humour; I cannot but look on it as a Womanish, or at best, a Pedantick one, but all I can do has hitherto been ineffectual; on the contrary, it encreases on me, and every Thing that moves up and down with any swift Motion before my Eyes, throws me into the Condition I so much dread. I have had the Advice of the best and most learned Physicians, who all agree, *That it proceeds from having so many Years accustomed myself to a Steadfastness of Sight, for the Sake of my Consulters.*

THOSE

THOSE who know the Fatigue I undergo from the Moment I rife out of my Bed, till I go into it again, will own, that I have enough to diftract the ftrongeft Head in the World: I am not only obliged to tell all forts of People their Names, Conditions, and future Events, but thofe of others whom they had any Bufinefs with. In fpite of my Regard for the fair Sex, I muft do Juftice to Truth, and own, they were infinitely the moft troublefome; they muft be told, whether *Maids, Wives, Widows,* or *Crack'd-Pipkins,* the Names of their Fathers, Mothers, Hufbands, Lovers, or Keepers; nay, I muft be pofitive to the very Days of firft, fecond, fometimes third Marriages, and frequently the Name and Difpofition of a Friend by the bye: If any one of thefe Articles are left unanfwered, my Confulter grouls like a Cat over a Piece of Lights, fays, *She has given her Money for nothing,* and plagues my Wife with fuch a Heap of Noife and Nonfenfe, that Deafnefs is a Bleffing to me. Scarce has one of thefe left the Houfe, but, probably, in comes a Cook-maid, fays, *Her filver Spoon is not come home yet; that I help'd fuch a one, and fuch a one to their loft Goods, and that I ufe her very ill:* Then enters two or three more, one has quarrelled with her Sweetheart laft Night, and I muft find another for her; a Second is jealous of her Hufband, I muft tell her what Whore he keeps Company with, that fhe may go and tear her Eyes out; in fhort, I am obliged to bear ten thousand Family Quarrels on my Shoulders, as if I were in the Fault of every Thing. Sometimes I have had thirteen or fourteen at a Time in my House, every one complaining of Haste, and pressing to be first answered, 'tis therefore more strange that I was able to satisfy any one of them, than that such a Multiplicity of different Affairs did not very much confound me; yet if I have failed in a Letter of a Name, or a Day in the Month, all the rest was nothing. I have frequently been plagued with People, who, after being resolved all the Questions in the Compass of my Art, were so Silly and Wicked as to expect to know Secrets, which the Divine Wisdom conceals from all Humane Penetration. Nay, some have desired I would have Recourse to Diabolical Arts, and force the Infernals to declare, what absent Persons were doing. I remember a Woman that wanted to have her Lover fetched from *Jamaica* through the Air. If I attempted to dissuade them from any Thoughts of such Practices, by Arguments drawn from Religion, they upbraided me with *Hypocrisy*, and told me, *They knew I dealt with the Devil, though I would not raise him for them:* If I assured them, that such Things were not in the Power of a Mortal, they called me *Impostor*, said, *I knew nothing of my Business; and they would go to those who had more Skill*. I leave it to the Judgment of any unprejudiced Reader, what a Hurry of Spirit this must put me in, and whether all this is not enough to occasion the

the Disorder I complain of, and which my Enemies so cruelly insinuate is but feigned. I shall hereafter give some Instances of the Usage I have met with on this Score, in the very Words I received it, not being ashamed to confess the Affronts given me, when with the same Impartiality and Truth, I also discover the Occasions of them.

But to return: I believe no Man ever had more Enemies, nor did less to create them. I have little Defence but my own Innocence; not but that I have Friends too, and among the noblest and most learned, but they think it Prudence to yield to Custom, and generally chuse rather to hear me traduced, than suffer themselves to be ridiculed, for offering any thing in my Vindication, by those *would-be Wits*, who pretend to be above giving Credit to any thing. Besides, it often happens that a Wife shall have experienced the Truth of my Predictions, yet dares not take my Part against her unbelieving Husband, lest he should take it ill she came to consult me. It is the same Case sometimes on the Husband's Side, who, though he does nothing without my Advice, dreads the Censure of his talkative Spouse, and therefore permits her to rail against me uninterrupted: Peace must be preserved in Families, whatever becomes of the poor Conjurer: But it would be endless to recount the various Particulars by which my Reputation suffers,

suffers, so I shall only say, *That while I live my chief Study must be Patience,* having nothing to console me under so many unjust Aspersions, but the Assurance, that when ever I dye, the Scandal thrown on me will die too, and my Memory obtain that which I despair of while in this World, a Publick Veneration and Love.

CHAP. III.

Some convincing PROOFS *that I always preferred the Interest of my* CONSULTERS *to my* OWN.

NOTHING has brought the Art of foretelling Events into more Contempt, than the exorbitant Desire of Gain, that most of the Professors of it testify. If they get but Money, they do not care how grosly soever they impose on those who rely on them; and a Person who sets up for a Fortune-teller, has little more to do, than to dive into the Humour and Inclination of his Consulters, which, once known, 'tis easy to flatter them with the Hope of Success in their Desires. It is in this I have chiefly distinguished myself from the common Herd. I could not see a Person, who asked my Advice, entering into any Affair, which would terminate in in his or her Undoing, without endeavouring to put a Stop to it; Things, in reality, the moſt deſtructive, often wear the moſt pleaſing Shape, and when I attempted to ſet them in their true Colours, have generally gained nothing by it but ill Will; whereas, had I flattered the Wiſhes of my Conſulter, I might have had my own Price; but I defy the whole World to charge me with a Deception of that Nature. When I foreſaw Ills that were unavoidable by Precaution, I have, indeed, forbore to ſhock ſuch Perſons with the Knowledge of them, remembering the old Proverb, that, *Sufficient for the Day is the Evil thereof*; but when Warnings were likely to be of any Effect, I never failed to give them in the plaineſt Manner I was able. And here I muſt take Notice, that the Planets which, under God, have the Direction of Human Incidents, do not always render infallible the Miſchief threatened by a malevolent Aſpect. Timely Care has ſometimes given the Lye to the moſt terrible Portents, as in the Caſe of the Merchant, mentioned in the Book of my Life, who had determined to lay violent Hands on himſelf, yet, through the Grace of God, and my Perſuaſions, was preſerved; various Inſtances of this kind are alſo related at full, in a Book intitled, *The Spy on the Conjurer*, which makes it needleſs to repeat them here. There are many living Witneſſes, and, I believe, will be when I am laid in the Earth, of my Tenderneſs, in revealing an inevitable ſad Fate. I had ſeveral People of Diſtinction

ſtinction with me, when a Lady, whom I had never ſeen before, came to make Tryal of my Art, ſhe was beautiful as an Angel, not exceeding eighteen Years of Age, and to all Appearance, in a State of perfect Health and Vigour; ſhe was about being married to a Gentleman who had courted her two Years, the Articles were drawn, and the Wedding-day fixed; her Queſtions were, *If he would be a good Huſband, and how many Children ſhe ſhould have:* I was very merry over a Bowl of Punch with my Friends, when this fair Lady arrived; but I had no ſooner caſt my Eye on her, than I fell into Agonies which no Tongue can reveal, nor Heart conceive, but thoſe, who, like me, are preſented with ſuch Objects, as the Gift of *Second Sight* affords, at the Preſence of a Perſon fated to a violent Death. She laid down her Guinea with her Queſtions, but I returned them both, and ſigned to my Wife to tell her, *That I was not in a Condition of doing any Buſineſs that Day.* She went away very much diſſatisfied, but left me more ſo. When ſhe was gone, I was aſked by ſome of the Company, *What had cauſed me to refuſe ſo fair a Lady's Money,* and were not a little merry on the Occaſion, till I told them, *That if they had ſeen what I did, they would be all ſad:* In fine, I acquainted them *for nothing,* with what I would not have revealed to her for *more Guineas than ſhe offered Shillings,* which was, *That ſhe would not live a Fortnight;* that by ſome Accident ſhe would

would be thrown off a Horse, her Brains dashed out, and her beautiful Body mangled and disfigured: This Prediction made them all shudder with Horror, and put an End to our Mirth for that Day. About the Time I mentioned, the News-Papers gave an Account of the Accident in the Manner I had foretold, which encreased the Regard of those who were Witnesses of my Behaviour in this Point, and convinced them, that I was an Enemy either to flattering or shocking my Consulters, as well as to deceiving them.

ANOTHER remarkable Instance of the same Kind happened on my being invited to a Marriage-Entertainment, where many of my good Friends being present, Mirth and the chearful Glass went round in great Abundance, till about Eight of the Clock at Night, two Gentlemen, who were invited Guests, but had been detained by some Affairs, came into the Room; one of them was middle-aged, but the other appeared not to exceed Nineteen or Twenty; I think my Eyes never beheld a more lovely Youth, nor one that had more the Air of a Man of Quality, as, indeed, he was, being the honourable Mr. *Hamilton*, Son of the Earl of *Abercorne*, of the Kingdom of *Ireland*; but scarce had I Time to contemplate his Beauties, when I saw him struggling amidst the tempestuous Waves, which seem'd to toss him to and fro, and at last came entirely over him, and hid him from any farther View: While this terrible Object presented itself before me, me, the young Gentleman was making his Compliments to the Company; I would have taken that Opportunity to have left the Room, but could not do it so timely but that I was seen, and prevented: My Disorder being taken Notice of, every-body desired to know the Reason, which I evaded by telling them on my Fingers, *That I was taken ill, and would go into the Air, but if I found myself better, would return*; tho', I must confess, I was far from intending to perform my Promise, my Concern for the poor young Gentleman not suffering me to do any thing that Night but lament his ill Fate. The next Morning I was visited by Mrs. *Hill*, who was one of the Company I mention'd, and a Lady extremely witty and facetious, but of the most inquisitive Disposition in the World; she imagined I had left the Company because of some private Pique I might have to one of the Gentlemen, and would not be brought from that Opinion till I told her the whole Truth; on which, she went immediately to one who was intimate with Mr. *Hamilton*, and acquainted him with what I said. He came to me in a few Days, and begged I would write down my Prediction, which he would shew him, in order to make him change his Design of embarking with Lord *Bellhaven*, and offered me a very great Consideration for so doing; but I knowing the Doom irrevocable, and that if he thought to escape it by putting off his intended Voyage, yet it would fall on him by some other Means, would not

be

be perſuaded either to write any thing to him, or ſee him: In a ſhort Time after he embarked, and, with a great many other noble and brave Men, was ſunk in the Abyſs of Waters.

I COULD give many more Proofs that I have refuſed Money, when by taking it I muſt be obliged to antedate Misfortunes, or deceive thoſe that were fated to ſuffer them, by vain Hopes; but theſe two are ſufficient to atteſt the Truth of my Principle, and I ſhall now proceed to ſome few Narrations for the Teſtification of the ſincere and diſintereſted Tenderneſs I had for all thoſe who applied to me in Diſtreſs.

I WAS, one Day, accoſted by two Gentlewomen, for ſuch the moſt ordinary Eye might diſcover them to be, by their Air and Mien, tho' very much out of Repair as to Habit; the younger of them ſeemed preſſed with a deep Melancholly, and laying down a Crown-Piece on the Table, wrote to me, *That it was all ſhe could ſpare at that Time, but begged I would not be a Niggard of my Study for her, tho' I might think by the Meanneſs of her Preſent, ſhe was ſo of her Purſe.* I aſſured her I would not, and letting the Money lie where it did, in a few Minutes wrote down the future Events which I ſaw would befal her: If I ſhould repeat what they were, few of my Readers but would know the Lady by the Extremes of her Fortune, which, being improper, I ſhall only ſay, *That ſhe was, at that Time,*

Time, in the moſt abjeᴄt Condition, and I promiſed her a Turn of Fate ſo great, and ſo unexpeᴄted, that I perceived the Credit ſhe appeared to give to it, was rather Complaiſance than Reality. As ſhe was preparing to take Leave, I put the Crown into her Hand, and ſpoke to my Wife on my Fingers, to bid her go Home and redeem the Word of God, which ſhe had no ſooner ſaid, than the poor Gentlewoman looked on her Friend with the utmoſt Amazement; but as ſoon as ſhe had recovered herſelf, ingenuoſly confeſſed, *That having nothing elſe wherewith to procure Money, ſhe had borrowed the Crown ſhe had given me, on her Bible*, and added, *That ſhe would do as I deſired, and whenever the good Fortune I had foretold, ſhould happen (which now ſhe did not in the leaſt doubt, ſince I had the Power of diſcovering what ſhe had intruſted no Mortal with) ſhe would make every Shilling I had ſo generouſly returned, five Guineas*. But here I had an Inſtance of the Forgetfulneſs and Ingratitude of the World; for in the Space of two Years afterwards, I ſaw this very Lady bowling in her Coach and Six by my Door every Day, but had never the Favour of a Viſit, or any Token of Remembrance from her.

Would I have entered into Meaſures to beguile my Conſulters, I have had frequent Opportunities by the Means of Mr. B———d, a Man of a good Family, the more the Pity he ſhould ſo far degenerate, he pretends to great Learning, but that I am not a Judge of; I know among
ignorant

ignorant People he is listened to as an Oracle, but, in my Opinion, that is chiefly owing to his Pretensions to Honour and good Nature, tho' never Man had less of either, in Reality; for he looks on all Mankind as his Property, deceives the Men for Interest, and abuses the Women for Diversion; I never knew him do a generous Thing by the one Sex, nor give any of the other a good Word, excepting one, who by the most vile Actions has drawn on her the Contempt of every-body besides. He never was intimate any-where, that he did not make it his first Business to set the Husband and Wife at Variance, and if ever his splenetick, I may say devilish, Humour can taste of Happiness, 'tis when he sees those most nearly ally'd, contriving each other's Destruction: I am no great Friend to Poetry, but I remember to have read somewhere, tho' I can neither quote the Book nor Author, this Line:

He, Devil-like, the Woes of Men enjoys.

But whoever wrote it, I am apt to fancy he was acquainted with Mr. B———d, who never smiles but when he makes others weep. He essayed all his Arts to set me against my Wife, and even while he was at Bed and Board with us, receiving all the Civilities we could treat him with, was still discontented, because he found it more difficult than ordinary to break that perfect Harmony between us: Failing in that, he insinuated himself into my Son's good Graces, and

and made him guilty of a Behaviour towards me, which required my utmost Indulgence to forgive. Yet this Man, this Hypocrite, takes the Name of the Great God a thousand Times a Day in his Mouth; to witness, *That he would rather rake the Kennels, than act against his Conscience*; he tells you, *He might have been employed by the Ministry, but would starve sooner than enter into any Measures contradictory to his Principles.* I must, indeed, acknowledge him a Lover of Justice, but 'tis in such a Way, as few would chuse to exert themselves in, which is this: He frequently goes out late at Night, especially in rainy Weather, and calls a Coach, always chusing the most jaded Horses he can find, then is drove to the longest Fare, tho' he has no manner of Business, but to try if the Coachman will demand more than the Act of Parliament allows, that he may have an Opportunity of complaining to the Commissioners: Nothing pleases him better than to see the poor Wives and Children of those Fellows come a-begging to him to be moderate, and if they sell their Beds to pay their Forfeit, the more exquisite his Delight. If he catches a Chair in the Path-way, he is sure to break the Glasses; or a Porter with a Burthen, to throw him down, knowing neither dare resent it, because he has the Law on his Side; but this he calls Honour, and a strict Reverence to the Statutes. Heaven forgive the Cruelty of his Nature, but sure Earth cannot parallel it since the Days of *Nero*; but why should I say *Nero*?
he

he burnt but one City, this Wretch would set the whole World into a Flame, if he had the Power. Never was a greater *Crocadile*, for with Humane Voice he drew the Ears of the Company to listen to his Persuasions, which are never made but to undo.

I HAVE been so particular in his Character, to shew how easy it would have been for me, if leagued with such a Man, to have made my own Fortune, and ruined Thousands.

AMONG the many whom he would feign have tempted me to join with him in the Undoing, were two Custom-House Officers, the Name of the one was *R. Loggins*, he was of a very advanced Age, and had enjoyed his Post above thirty Years; the other, who was called *J. Rotherham*, was much younger, but had been a considerable Time in the Business. He found they had saved a little Money, and were of projecting Dispositions, though of mean Capacities to manage any great Affair. He had told them, *'Twas easy for them to prove the King was wronged in his Revenue of the Customs*, and set them to Work to calculate what their Whimsies improved by his own might amount to, which, I think, they brought in upwards of 30,000*l.* a Year: He made them believe they should have ten thousand Pounds a-Piece for the Discovery, and would have prevailed on me to tell them, *I foresaw, by my Art, that they would have great Rewards*. I did not

not abfolutely deny what he defired, and bad him bring them to me, though not with any Defign to aid his Purpofe, but to fave, if it were in my Power, the poor Fellows from Ruin. When they came, I told them, *I had but little Skill in Schemes of that Nature, but knew the World too well to promife them Succefs* ; *'tis like ftopping the Tide at* Gravefend *with your Thumb,* faid I to *Loggins* ; though, by the way, this was none of my own Wit, but a Comparifon made on a certain Occafion, by a Peer in Parliament. *Rotherham,* blown up with the Hopes *B——d* had given him, wrote with a pert Air, *What do you think of me ?* I anfwered him, *That he would ftarve in a Prifon, if he purfued his prefent Defign* ; *that the Perfons he would be obliged to Accufe were too powerful for a thoufand fuch Enemies as he, or his Friend.* To this he replied with an Oath, *That he would write to the King himfelf,* and prefently took Paper, and began to do as he had fworn, in, as near as I can remember, thefe Words.

To the KING.

SIR,

WE have no Justice from your Ministry: I beg to speak to your Majesty myself, that I may inform you, by Word of Mouth, what cheating Knaves you have got in your Custom-House.

I am,

Your MAJESTY's

Subject and humble Servant,

J. ROTHERHAM.

To this fine Epistle he added a Postcript, where the King should direct to him; I forgot the Name of the Alley, but it was somewhere behind St. *Paul*'s Church. To this extravagant Pitch had Mr. B―――d's Insinuations wound up the Expectations of these unfortunate Men, and all I could do to warn them of their Folly, was to no more Purpose, than to throw Water against the Wind. I soon after heard the younger Hero was put into *New-Prison*, some-body having sworn Treason against him; and poor *Loggins*, after having spent all his own Money, and a hundred Pounds borrowed, I saw begging with his Grey Hairs at a Door, to my great Concern, on the Account of his Age.

NOR

Nor was I less troubled at the Misfortunes to which Mr. *Rogers*, a Baker, was reduced by the Artifices of this general Deceiver, who so far intoxicated him, by telling him, *He was a Wit, and should join with him in writing a Weekly Paper*, that he neglected his Business, spent all his Time and Money among Printers, Publishers, and Paper Merchants, put his Wife into *Bedlam*, for having Prudence enough to dislike Mr. B—d, and the Measures he made him take, and was afterwards turned out of Doors by his Landlord, all his Goods seized on, and he glad to be a Journeyman, and a Slave for Life, who before lived in good Repute. From the Time he began to sink, Mr. B——d used him as the Devil does the Witch, never came near him, but made a Jest of his Calamities. I have many Witnesses of the Warnings I gave this Man, but to as little Purpose as those I bestowed on the *Custom-House* Officers : He comes sometimes to my House to this Day, and laments the little Regard he pay'd to my Advice, and curses B———d in the utmost Bitterness of his Soul.

'Tis certain, that no Rank nor Degree, but was liable to be ensnared by him. Mr. *Hughs*, a Non-juring Clergyman, and exceeded by few, in good Sense and Learning, could not defend himself from giving into a Project he proposed to him ; in which having spent all he had, and reduced himself to great Miseries, in the End broke his Heart.

I

I fear I have been already too tedious in thofe melancholly Accounts; but I am oblig'd, in the Vindication of my Character, to relate them that the Reader may be convinced, how little I regarded my Intereft, when it depended on doing a Prejudice to thofe who confulted me, fince by foothing any of thofe Perfons I have named, and Numbers of others not mentioned, whom Mr. B———d brought to me, I might have been one of the greateft Gainers by their Lofs.

But though I fhould publifh thefe, and ten thoufand more Inftances of this Nature, fo prejudiced are fome People, that it would all pafs for nothing; and to the reft of my Accufations, I doubt not, Oftentation would be added; for which Reafon, among others, I refolve to let no Perfon in the World perufe this Manufcript, till I am beyond the Reach of Envy or of Malice. I cannot, however, in Juftice to thofe worthy Perfons, who have not difdained appearing in Behalf of the *Dumb Conjurer*, omit making mention of fome Inftances that I had Friends as well as Enemies; among the Number of them was my good Lady *Afhfield*, who was not only famous for her Beauty, Riches, and Honour, but had alfo all the rare Qualities that can be found in Woman. I foretold fome extraordinary Events, to a lovely Daughter of hers, which happened exactly according to my Predictions, tho' nothing at that Time feem'd more unlikely.

D   She

She used to send frequently for me, and take me Abroad with her to all Places where she was free. Another Instance, that all Mankind were not set against me, I met with at the Playhouse in *Drury-Lane*, one Night, when that excellent Comedy, *The Provoked Wife*, was acting. My Wife would needs have me accompany her, as imagining, perhaps, that no-body had so much Reason to be provoked as herself. About the Middle of the Third Act, three Sparks, whom I had seen at my Lady *Ashfield*'s, and who had rally'd her Ladyship, on the Confidence she put in me, came into the Pit, and immediately attacked both me and my Wife: I was very busy on my Finger-Discourse with Mr. *Beston* and *Claudy Philips*, two famous Hands on the Violin, and did not regard the Behaviour of these Fops, till one of them damning us all, and what we were about: I perceived *Claudy* made some Answer to him, on which another of them said, as I was afterwards informed, *That if I did not go out of the House, he would have me kick'd out. By Heaven!* replyed *Beston*, *You had better be quiet, lest you meet with the same Fate, for he is not a Man who will bear an Insult if he knows of it.* *Claudy*, at whose Mother's House I lodged, and loved me as his Life, made known to me, on his Fingers, all this Hero said; on which I turned about, and finding the other two Sparks, his Companions, busy about my Wife: I had no longer Patience, but knock'd the first Beaux off his Seat; they all three immediately drew, and so,

indeed,

indeed, did   who knew
me very well, and saw the Danger I was in, tho'
he was in the Middle of his Part, leap'd off the
Stage, and put his Arms about my Neck, and
in that Posture, assisted by some other of the
Actors, carried me behind the Scenes, where,
getting a Pen and Ink, I wrote a Challenge, having learned his Name, to him, who seemed the
Chief of this Heroick Band. My Lord *Ilay*
came in to me while I was writing, would needs
be the Bearer of it himself, and protested he
would be my Second; doing me the Honour to
say, *That* Duncan Campbel *was his Relation, and
as good a Gentleman as any there.* I was carried
that Night to St. *Amant's* Coffee-House, in St.
Martins-Lane, where was a Club of Gentlemen
of the Army: On their being informed of the
Story, a Consultation was held, in what Manner
to chastise the Spark, in Case he did not answer my
Apointment; one was for having him *Posted in
all publick Places for a Coward*; a Second, for
having him *well Bastinadoed*; but a Third, more
moderate, said, *That, as he was a Beaux, a little
Switch to beat the Powder out of his Wig, would
answer the End, as well as knocking his Brains out.*
While I was thus diverting myself with good
Company and *Arrack* Punch, my Adversary was
employ'd with Lawyers to indict me in the *Crown
Office*, on the Statute against Gypsies, Fortune-
tellers, Witches, &c.———of which I had early Notice next Morning, by Mrs. *Storys* of *Nor-
folk-Street.* I, who knew nothing what the

Crown-Office meant, shewed her a Paper I was resolved to stick up in all the Coffee-Houses about Town, the Gentleman not having met me; but she begg'd I would defer it till Three o' Clock, when she would bring the Lawyer to me, that it might be made up. I could not refuse a fair Lady; and Providence, who had preserved me in many Dangers, was here particularly careful of me; for my old Friend, Justice *Botelar* of *West-minster*, came to dine with me that Day, and tarrying till the Lawyer came, heard him insist, *That I should ask Pardon, on my Knees, of the Gentleman:* But he no sooner heard his Name, than he started up, and shaking his Cane, *Go, tell the Rogue*, said he, *that he is my Nephew; that I saved him but the other Day from* Newgate, *and if I ever hear he meddles with my Friend,* Campbel, *I'll send him thither.* The Lawyer on this departed, and I had no farther Trouble about the Business.

CHAP.

CHAP. IV.

On WITCHCRAFT.

NOTHING is more surprising to me, than that Persons of Sense, especially a *Religious* one, should run on with that Vehemence, as some do, against all Accounts of *Witchcraft*: The Holy Scripture, both in the *Old* and *New Testament*, affords Variety of Texts to prove it; but lest they would not be thought to disbelieve any Part of what is there contained, they have found out this *Salvo*; to wit, *That there was such Things in the* Jewish *Times, but they were all abolished by the Sufferings of our Blessed Saviour*: I know not what Reason they give for it, besides their own Imagination, for I never read that he has told us so.

IF there has been none who have practised *Witchcraft* of late Years, how highly must those Judges be blamed, who have sentenced so many to the Stake, as were burned both in *Scotland*, and the North of *England*, in the Years 1627, and 1629. Since then many have suffered for the same Crime, though not in such great Numbers; and that there still are Persons guilty of it, may be proved by those unfortunate Creatures who feel the Effects of it, in a Manner, which no Distemper, to which Humane Nature is incident, can inflict on them; though to have made a Contract with the Devil, and receive from him the Power of doing Hurt, is now looked on as such an old Wife's Tale, that if any Person is apprehended for it, a Justice of the Peace is afraid to sign a Commitment, tho' on the most plain Proofs, for Fear of being laugh'd at by those, Wise in their own Conceit, Gentlemen, who will have it no more than Imagination.

But if there be no such Thing as *Witchcraft*, what is that terrible Condition to which many People have been, and are, reduced to? Why does it puzzle the Art of the whole College of Physicians? Why is it never in the Power of Physick to make a Cure, or even give the least Ease to the Persons afflicted? What is it gives that supernatural Strength to the unhappy Wretch, that, tho' a Child of not above seven or eight Years of Age, a Dozen Men shall not be able to hold him? Every-body knows that, in ordinary Diseases, the sick Person becomes Weak: What conveys into the Stomach Pins, Needles, Bundles of Hair, Sticks, Straws, and other Things, which I have seen vomited up? What is it that makes them speak in Voices not their own, and talk learnedly on Things they know nothing of?

There

There is no accounting for it but by diabolical Practices, what, in old Times, bore the Name of *Inchantment*, and is now vulgarly called *Witchcraft*. I had a Man brought to me about twelve Years since, whose Head was turned directly behind him, all his Limbs distorted, and the sadest Spectacle to behold, that Imagination can possibly form; he had ruined himself by following the Prescriptions of divers Physicians before he came to me; but his Case will best be described by his own Affidavit, made before the Lord Chief Justice *Raymond*, which I here incert for that Purpose.

The AFFIDAVIT *of* RICHARD COATES, *Vintner.*

RICHARD COATES, *late of Fenchurch-Street, Vintner, and Citizen of London, maketh Oath, That he, this Deponent, was for above four Years, afflicted with a violent Distemper, which was by most People judged to be the Effect of Witchcraft; his Head and all his Limbs being distorted, and drawn into very strange and unnatural Postures: Whereupon this Deponent applied himself to several eminent Physicians for their Assistance therein, and in particular to the late Dr. Ratcliffe and Dr. Cade, who, after this Deponent had been under their Hands for upwards of four Years, sent him to the* Bath *for a Cure, but without any Effect; which, and his long languishing under the said Distemper, cost him upwards of Five*

Hundred *Pounds*, *besides the Ruin of his Trade in his Calling of an Wholesale Tobacconist; notwithstanding all which, he found no Relief, but grew still worse: upon which, this Deponent, hearing of one Mr.* Duncan Campbel, *and being made sensible of many surprizing Cures which he had performed, as set forth in the History of the said* Campbel's *Life; he, this Deponent, applied himself to the said* Duncan Campbel, *for his Advice and Assistance in the said Distemper; who, in a few Months, by God's Blessing, perfectly cured this Deponent thereof; insomuch that this Deponent hath ever since (being about ten Years) been blessed with a very good State of Health, and been totally freed from the said Distemper,*

RICHARD COATES.

Jurat 8. *Jan.* 1725. apud
Serjeants-Inn, in *Chancery-Lane*, coram me
R. RAYMOND.

THIS is a Testimonial which no-body will dare to doubt the Truth of; and several of the like Nature were made before *Thomas Botelar*, Esq; one of his Majesty's Justices of the Peace for *Westminster*. What I did in these Cases were esteemed Miracles. I became so famous for the many Cures I did, that People, who had the least Reason to imagine themselves under an ill Tongue, would entreat me to lay my Hands on them, if I did no more; believing there was
Virtue

Virtue enough, even in a Touch of mine, to remove whatever Malignity they laboured under.

THERE was one Patient I had, which I cannot forbear making Mention of; she was the Daughter of a Farmer, and seized in a strange Manner as she was going to *Rumford* Market, her Limbs distorted, and the Use of her Senses taken away: Her Parents were greatly afflicted, and sent her to *London* for the Physicians Advice. The House she was at, belonged to a Relation of her Mother, and was a Potter in *Tooly-Street, Southwark*; she remained there some Time, and no Money was spared in order to recover her: Doctors, Surgeons, and Apothecaries were consulted, but none of them knew what to make of her Distemper. I was her last Resource, and had no sooner cast my Eye on her, than I knew the Cause by which she was aggrieved, and told the Company, *that she was bewitched*; on which, one of them presently cried out, *That she believed it was so, for she had heard the Girl often say, she could not be quiet for an old Woman, and that she would point to a Corner of the Room, and say she stood there, and seemed very angry no-body else could see her.* They begged me to use my utmost Endeavours for her, which I promised, and at the same Time assured them, that I did not doubt, with God's Assistance, making a perfect Cure in a short Time. Accordingly I used Means to bring the Witch to *London*; and when I knew what I had done would

prove

prove effectual, I went to the House where she was, and told the People, *I would not depart till I had left their Cousin as well as ever she was in her Life.* They looked on me with Astonishment, as not being able to believe it possible for me to make good my Words, she being still as bad as when I first saw her: I bad them *have Patience, and mark the End,* but said, *It would be Midnight before any thing could be done.* As I had told them, the Clock had not struck Twelve many Minutes, before they heard somebody knock at the Door; they would have opened it, but I forbad them, till after the third Knock, which being given, I made the Girl herself, and all the Family, go down with me, who were Witnesses, that as soon as I had opened the Door, an ill-favour'd old Woman, who stood before it, fell down on her Knees to me, and begged I would give her Leave to return. The young Woman immediately shriek'd, and said, *That was the Woman who haunted her Day and Night, and tormented her.* On which, the vile Wretch redoubled her Prayers, that I would release her: I knew my Work was done, and unloosed the Spell that had compelled her to come thither, by giving her a small Blow with my Cane. After this, we went into the House again, and my Patient was perfectly recovered, and could now tell us, *That as she was going to Market, she met this Woman, who, on her refusing to give her a Couple of Eggs that she begged of her, told her, it should be worse for her; then went away muttering something which she did not under-*

underſtand, but was that Minute ſeized in the Manner before deſcribed. The Relations of this Girl have often call'd upon me when they came on this Side the Water, and informed me, *That ſhe has never relapſed, and is ſince married, and has ſeveral Children.* This Cure I performed about fifteen Years ago.

I SHOULD be too tedious in attempting to relate the twentieth Part of the Number of Children to whom I have been ſerviceable, even tho' they were reduced ſo low by the Force of an ill Tongue, as to be looked upon as Changelings; I ſhall, therefore, trouble my Reader only with one which has ſomething ſo aſtoniſhing in its Circumſtances, as, I flatter myſelf, will excite no leſs Pleaſure than Surprize.

IT was the only Daughter of Mr. *Tiveſton*, a Gentleman of a competent Eſtate in *Berkſhire*; ſhe was about three Years old, and a peculiar Favourite, not only for being one of the moſt beautiful Infants in the World, but becauſe ſhe was the laſt Pledge of a moſt dear and tenderly beloved and loving Wife, who died in bringing her into the World. This Child was, one Day, at Play before the Door with her Nurſe, when an old Woman aſked her for a Piece of Cake ſhe had in her Hand, which ſhe not readily giving, the Witch gave three Strokes on the Ground with a Stick ſhe leaned on, and cried out as loud as ſhe could, *Meeli! Mali! Meeli!* for ſeveral Times

Times together, and then run away as swiftly as a Girl of Fifteen; tho' the Nurse, who gave this Account, said, *She appeared to be near a Hundred, and seemed so decrepid before, as tho' she could scarce creep along.* The Moment she was out of Sight, the Child began to cry, and presently after, the Noise she made could be compared to nothing but the Mewing of a Cat; in short, from that Time the Use of Speech was taken away; her pretty innocent Prattle, and the many little Actions which so much endear those of her Age to Parents, was now changed into a Behaviour far different; she crawl'd upon all Four; she spit upon every-body that offered to touch her, and on the Nurse's dressing or undressing her, fell into such Passions, that she even foamed at the Mouth. Never Trouble exceeded that of poor Mr. *Tiverton*; after having had Recourse to all the Help the Country afforded, he brought her to Town, but with as little Success, tho', as he told me himself, it had cost him more than three hundred Pounds. Mrs. *Mason*, my good Friend, at last advised him to me; he came, and brought the Child, the Cause of whose Misfortune I presently perceived, and described in a Bit of Paper the very Picture of the Wretch who had laid the cursed Spell upon her, as the Nurse, who still attended her, confessed. As the Accident happened in *Berkshire*, I found it very difficult to work a Cure here; for this pernicious Agent of Hell had made Use of other Means, I found, than the Witch who had afflicted the *Rumford* Maid,

Maid, and it was not in my Power to bring her to *London*, as I had done the other; nor would Mr. *Tiverton*'s Circumstances allow him to make me a Gratification for going to *Berkshire*, proportionable to the Loss it would have been to my Family, that I should be so long absent from *London*. I gave him, however, a Paper sealed up, which I ordered should be half stuck in the Ground, and the other half out, just in the Place, as near as the Nurse could remember, where the Witch had stood at the Time of her speaking to the Child: This I strictly charged should not be moved by any Person belonging to him; and to prevent a Stranger, who might accidentally pass that Way, from plucking it out, I desired he would place a Servant, Night and Day, to watch it: My Advice was punctually followed, and he wrote to me to inform me, that the third Night an old Woman was seen to hanker about the Place, but the Vigilance of the Servants preventing her from touching the Paper, she came the next Day, and begg'd she might see the Child, which she being, according to my Orders, permitted, she uttered, in a low Voice, some unintelligible Words, and went out of the House with the utmost Speed: From that Moment the poor Babe recovered her former Accents and Behaviour, to the Surprize of the whole Country, and the inexpressible Joy of her Father, who did not fail to send me an immediate Account of the Success of my Prescription, and the Reward agreed for between us, if it had

the

the defired Effect; which, I confefs, I did not greatly depend on myfelf, unlefs I could have been there in Perfon, fo ftrong was the diabolical Influence over her. Yet, thro' the merciful Affiftance of gracious Providence, the Myfteries of Hell were unravelled, and my little Patient perfectly reftored, and remained fo to her Death, which happened fome Years afterwards, of the Small-Pox.

Numberless are the Teftimonials may be given, that there are ftill Wretches on Earth fo abandon'd as to fell their Eternal Happinefs hereafter, for the vile Satisfaction they take in doing Mifchief; and I fincerely wifh, that thofe Perfons who are of a different Opinion, may never be convinced by wofully experiencing the Effects on themfelves of what they give fo little Credit to on others.

CHAP.

CHAP. V.

On the VARIOUS DECEPTIONS *endeavoured to be put on Me.*

MY telling Names at first Sight, appears so prodigious a Thing to all the World, that it is not surprising many who have not been assured of it themselves, should doubt the Truth of it, when told it by others. Nor do I blame the Caution of those Persons who refuse their Faith to every Thing (excepting the Divine Mysteries) that is not to be accounted for by Reason. The *Second Sight* is an Inspiration wholly Supernatural, and none but those really possest of it, can form any Idea what it is: therefore the Wonders wrought by it, may well seem Fabulous to those who prove 'em not. Those who were too much prejudiced to make the Tryal, have rendered what I pretend to this Way, a Handle to asperse me with the Title of an *Imposture*: Others, of a more candid Disposition, have thought fit to *prove* before they judged; and after having done so, have thought nothing too much to do for me, to attone for their past Diffidence: Of this Number was
the

the late Dutchefs of *Wharton*, who, on the 28th of *May*, 1723, when all the World were paying their Compliments at St. *James*'s, took that Opportunity to divert herfelf with the pretended *Conjurer*, (as fhe thought) or at leaft to fatisfy herfelf, whether I was fuch or not.

ACCORDINGLY fhe came with her Nurfe and Woman, but more meanly habited than either of them: I was gone to take my Morning Walk in the Park, when this Vifit was made; but my Wife telling them that I would return foon, they confented to ftay, though not without fome Difficulty. They told her, *That they were all Servants in one Family, and fhould get Anger if miffed.* The Nurfe paffed for the Houfekeeper, the Dutchefs for Chambermaid, and her Woman for Cook.

As I happened to ftay that Morning fomewhat longer than ordinary, my Wife met me upon the Stair-Cafe, and told me on her Fingers, *The Devil was in me to run about fo and neglect my Bufinefs; that there was three Servants had waited for me an Hour and a Half, and fhe had much ado to perfuade them to ftay.* I made her no Anfwer, but threw off my Great-Coat, and went into the Room. They had all wrote their feveral Queftions ready for me.

The

The Dutchess's was as follows.

SIR, I have a very good Place, tho' my Lady is somewhat peevish, and my Lord's Gentleman is very much my Enemy, and has made a thousand Lies on me, so that I am threatened to be turned away every Hour. I desire to know if he will get his Ends or not. Pray be speedy, for if my Lady, who is now Abroad, should come Home, and I out of the Way, I must not expect to lie another Night in the House.

The Nurse wrote in this Manner.

SIR, I have a Son at Sea, a wild Youth, but very Ingenious: I would know if he will come Home safe, and what Time I may expect him, and if he will make a good Voyage.

The Woman wrote no more than these Words.

SIR, I have no particular Question, but desire to know, in general, if I am designed to a good or bad Fate.

I read their Papers, and then made a Sign, that she who would be first answered should go up; on which there was a great Dispute, who should have the Preheminence; but at length yielded to the seeming Housekeeper, both on the Account of her Age, and being upper Servant: But this Contest giving me an Opportunity of looking more stedfastly on them, than I usually do, till they go up, and I have placed myself in a fit Position

Position, I saw enough to know they were putting a Trick upon me; and, therefore, taking the Dutchess by the Hand, I, in a Manner, compelled her to take the Precedence. I was not many Minutes above with her, before I answered her Question in these Terms.

YOU serve no Lady, but a Lord, who, tho' the most accomplished and wittiest Man of the Age, has Humours which take away all the Happiness of Grandeur: Those Women below are your Attendants, but taste more Felicity than your Grace, because they have only the Pleasure of the best of Women to consult; you have that of the most capricious of Men.

THE Dutchess had no sooner read this than she turned as pale as Death, trembled, and had all the Symptoms of an approaching Swoon. I knew it was occasioned only by her Surprize, and that she would soon recover; but thinking it might be a Prejudice to her, she being young with Child, I stamped for my Wife, who run for a Bottle of Spirits, and some fair Water; the Women below, hearing the Noise, followed her, and by their Assiduities about the Indisposed, made my Wife know she was more than their Equal.

WHEN she came to herself, she shewed the Paper I had wrote, and ingenuously confess'd, *She came to try my Skill, not believing it possible I could*

could do the Things I pretended to; but she was now convinced that I was more than even my best Friends could represent me. The Women were in the utmost Astonishment, and looked on me as a kind of Prodigy.

After this, she proceeded to ask me several Questions, not only concerning herself and the Duke, but also of Matters relating to the State, to which I returned such Answers, as more assured her I was enabled to do it by no Intelligence, but an intellectual One.

I had the Honour of her Grace's Company almost the whole Day, my Lord Duke being at that Time out of Town; and I have been since informed, that she shewed him several of my Papers, and that the frequent Visits she made me afterwards, were as much by his Desire as her own; and, I believe, I may say, without Vanity, that the Alteration in his Conduct towards her, so much for the better, was owing to what I wrote.

Just such another Artifice, immediately after this, was practised on me by a young Lady, who, tho' not yet arrived to a Title, will not long be without one, and may be said to merit the noblest, if Virtue, Wit, good Humour, and the most perfect Beauty Nature ever made, can do it.

SHE came to me in a plain Stuff Gown, a coarse Housewife's Apron, and a round-ear'd Cap; the Person who accompanied her, was habited in much the same Manner, but neither so Young nor so Handsome by many Degrees; she seemed, however, to an ordinary Eye, to be the Superior of the two, and accordingly presented her Question first; but I presently saw thro' the Deception, and pushing her away, took the young Beauty and placed her in an Easy-Chair, and pointed to the other to stand behind it, taking, at the same Time, a Whip in my Hand, which always hangs by the Chimney in my Dining-Room, in order to keep the Dogs in Subjection, and smacked it several Times. The Astonishment they were both in is not to be expressed; but I took my Pen, and wrote in this Manner.

'TIS not the Habit can deceive me; I see the Person as it is, and regard not the outward Ornaments. You, young Charmer, are at present distinguished by the World only for your Beauty and good Qualities, but in a little Time will lose the Name of fine Mrs. ———, *for my Lady* ——— *You, who wanted to know your Fortune first, have already made it, by being Servant to so good a Mistress, and marrying the Coachman, who is a very honest Man, and by whom you are now with Child of a Girl.*

If

IF they were amazed before, they were now much more fo; and finding it in vain to continue their Difguife, frankly owned it, and afked my Pardon. I told them, *I was far from condemning fo innocent a Fraud*; nay, on the contrary, *wifhed that all who had the leaft Diffidence in me, would take the fame Meafures to be convinced*. I then related to them many Endeavours of the like kind to deceive and pofe me, with my Difcoveries of them, which very much diverted the young Lady, who fent for a Bottle of *French* Wine, and a Piece of *Salmon*, and was heartily merry for three or four Hours.

DID I not fear it might draw Reflections on fome of my fair Confulters, I could recount a Number who made ufe of thofe Stratagems, particularly, a certain Countefs, who, being a *Brunetta*, and of the largeft Size for her Sex, thought to deceive me, by coming in the Habit of the other; the Wife of a Baronet, who coloured her Face, and Neck, and wore a Jacket and Petticoat, in order to pafs on me for a *Molotta* Slave; but I chufe rather to lofe the Honour of being able to difcover the true Perfon from the Counterfeit, than make any Mention of thofe Perfons real Names, to whom it would be a Prejudice, and to give them feigned ones, would make this, which is in every Particular a true Hiftory, favour of Romance.

But I think it not so strange, that Women, to whom Curiosity is inherent, should take this extraordinary Pains, as I do at that of the Men: If they believe me an Impostor, or an ignorant Pretender, let them enjoy their Opinion, I never did, nor never will, give myself any Trouble to confute it; 'tis enough for me to please those who confide in me: In that my Ambition is satisfied, and I would chuse rather to be Easy than Great. But I have very good Reasons to be assured, that those Gentlemen who have endeavoured to find me out, as they call it, took not that Pains meerly to expose me, as they pretended, and to undeceive the World, but to consult me themselves, in case I should be found not deficient. So much is the Desire of being informed of future Events grafted in the Soul, that none, of whatever Sex, but would prefer that Knowledge to any other.

Every-body who has been with me, knows that when I have any very difficult Questions put to me, I go into the Air, leaving my Consulter alone for sometimes half an Hour, more or less, according as the Inspiration comes upon me, and enables me to give a Solution. I was one Day going on one of these little Progresses, when I was saluted at my Door by three Gentlemen, whose Habit and Deportment bespoke them to be Persons of Distinction. As they understood not the Finger Talk, I whistled for my Wife

to

to come down and know their Commands, to whom one of them said, *He was my Countryman, and that the others were of the Court of* France, *and just arrived here, but that the Fame of the wonderful Things I had done had reached their Ears, and, they believed, were not unknown to all the polite Courts of* Europe : *That this Visit was only intended to pay a Compliment to a Man so justly esteemed.* My Wife then told them, *That Ladies being in the House, who were averse to seeing any of their Sex, except him they came to consult, it was impossible for me to receive the Honour they did me, but in an Hour or two I should be free from other Company, and would then devote myself to them entirely.* All this being in an ill Light, my Door standing under an Arch, I could not distinguish the Physiognomy of any of those that spoke; but they were not gone half a Minute, before my good Genius informed me, this was no friendly Visitation, and bad me stand upon my Guard when they should return, as they promised to do at the Time prefixed by my Wife. As she had promised, however, that I would give them my Company, I would not avoid seeing them, and accordingly dispatched my Ladies with all the Speed I could, that I might be ready to receive them. They failed not to come, and after a Cup or two of Punch, began to put several Questions to me in a ludicrous Way, to all which I gave this general Answer.

Gentlemen, *for such I know you are, not by your Habit, but my own innate Intelligence, if you come with a real Desire of being inform'd of any thing within the Compass of my Art, I shall do my Best to satisfy you; or if you aim only at being diverted, I am as ready to promote Mirth as yourselves: But would beg you to remember I am a Gentleman also, and as I never offend against the Rules of good Manners, expect the same Decorum to be used towards me.*

Having delivered this to them with a serious Air, I observed them to look on one another with some Confusion, and, at length, freely own'd, That they came with no other Design than to banter me, but my Behaviour convincing them I was not the Person I had been represented, they acknowledged their Error, and should be glad of a farther Acquaintance. I then gave them to understand I knew they were all *Englishmen*; and, without a Fee, wrote several Hints to each of them, which let them see I was no Impostor, and had it in my Power to reveal what most they desired should be kept secret. The Conversation was, however, maintained with the utmost good Humour, and innocent Pleasantry, amongst us, for the whole Evening; after which, they took Leave, assuring me, *They would hear nothing spoken to my Disadvantage for the future, by any Person in their Company.* I have had, since, good Reason to believe what they said, having received many signal Favours

vours from all three, but especially from one, who, I must own, has been the best and sincerest Friend I ever met with.

Inexpressibly difficult have been the Tasks I have had put upon me, and had I fail'd in any one of them, as I must have done if my good Angel had not been extremely watchful on those Occasions, it would have passed current in the World, *that I was an Impostor.* For Instance, a Gentleman of great Worth and Honour, and my very good Friend and Champion, happened one Day into some Company, where I was made the Subject of the utmost Ridicule; one seemed more inveterate than the rest, and said, *He knew I could not tell any Person's Name, without being first informed of it by some Spy or other*; adding, *That he knew I kept a Pack of Vagabond Fellows on purpose to watch Home those who came to consult me.* My Friend, who was entirely satisfied of the contrary, offered to lay a Wager of twenty Guineas on my Head, that I would tell the Name of any Person he should bring to me; the other readily took him up, but on this Condition, that it should be one who was a Stranger to all the Company. My Defender agreed, and to make the Matter more sure, they all adjourn'd that Afternoon to an adjacent Tavern, whence my Friend, by Consent of them all, wrote me a Line, desiring to speak with me that Moment, on extraordinary Business, but made no Mention of what Nature: I was a little indisposed when

the

the Porter brought this Letter to me, but having a great Regard for the Gentleman that sent it, dress'd myself, and complied immediately with his Summons. I was not a little surprized to find so great a Number of fine Ladies and Gentlemen with him, there being thirteen in Number. I had not been long sat down, before my Friend told me, *I was to tell the Name of a Person I should see in a little while :* On which, I began to excuse myself on Account of my Indisposition, for, indeed, I was not in a Humour for Business at that Time. I had no sooner seem'd to evade it, but I perceived a malicious Smile sit on the Faces of all the Company, except my Friend, who appeared as much displeased, and wrote again, *That he had laid a Wager on my Head, and if I did not perform now, as usual, he should have Reason to take it ill :* On which, I return'd, *That to oblige him, and vindicate my own Honour, I would do much.* I then desired to know, *Which of those Strangers, for they were all such to me, I was to try my Art upon :* But they would not consent it should be any that was known to my Friend, lest by some private Token he might inform me. It was, at last, agreed, that two of the Gentlemen should stand at the Door, and desire the first Person that came by, and seem'd to have Sense enough not to be displeased at the Jest, to come in. This was accordingly done, and they brought in a Man of about fifty Years of Age. I must confess, I was much longer before I satisfied the Curiosity of these People, than ordinary,

ordinary, the Compulsion, as it were, that was put on me, the Witticisms I perceived were made by my Adversaries, and the Impatience of my Friend, involved me in Thoughts not at all to the Furtherance of what I was to do. I accomplish'd it, however, tho' this Person had three Names, and very uncommon ones, *viz. Azariah Tomlinson Blackenthorp*, which I wrote down in the same Manner, not missing one Letter, as he himself confessed, as he spelled them: He, moreover, told the Company, *That he was an* American *born, and was never in* England *more than a Month at a Time in three or four Years; so that it was impossible Chance should ever have made us acquainted.*

My Friend now triumph'd, and the others look'd as much confused as they had been gay before; they did not fail, however, to treat me with the utmost Civility, and I had, afterwards, Visits from them all; the very Person who laid the Wager against me, doing nothing, from that Time, without my Advice.

I had another Tryal, of much the same Nature with this, put upon me: It was to tell the Name of a Boy, who came a hundred Miles Distance, to serve in a Coffee-House, and was arrived but the Moment they sent for me, nor had told his Name to any Person but his Master: This Affair terminated to my Advantage and Honour, a great many Gentlemen of the best Fashion,

Fashion, as well as others, being present when I fulfilled the Request made to me.

Many more of these Examples could I give my Reader, but I chuse to confine myself to a few which have happened of late Years, and yet fresh in the Memory of my Friends; and are sufficient to prove my Art is not to be deceived by any Stratagems whatsoever.

CHAP. VI.

On Omens: *Which are to be depended on, and which not.*

NOTHING is more contrary to good Sense, than imagining every thing we see and hear is a Prognostick either of Good or Evil, except it be the Belief that nothing is so. I have known People who have been put into such terrible Apprehensions of Death by the squeaking of a Weazel, as have been very near bringing on them the Fate they dreaded. Others have thought themselves secure of receiving Money, if their Hands itched, or, by chance, a little Spider fell upon their Cloaths: Some will defer going Abroad, tho'

tho' called by Business of the greatest Consequence, if, happening to look out of the Window, they see a single Crow; or going out, are met by a Person who has the Misfortune to squint; either of these turns 'em immediately back, and, perhaps, by delaying till another Time what requires an immediate Dispatch, the Affair goes wrong, and the Omen is, indeed, fulfill'd, which, but for the Superstition of the Observer, would have been of no Effect.

How many People have I seen in the most terrible Palpitations, for Months together, expecting, every Hour, the Approach of some Calamity, only by a little Worm which breeds in old Wainscot, and endeavouring to eat its Way out, makes a Noise like the Movement of a Watch. Others again, by having caught Cold, feel a certain Noise in their Heads, which seems to them like the Sound of distant Bells, fancy themselves warned of some great Misfortune.

The Fire also affords a kind of Divination to these Omen-mongers; they see Swords, Guns, Castles, Churches, Prisons, Coffins, Wedding-Rings, Bags of Money, Men and Women, or whatever ehey either fear or wish, plainly decyphered in the glowing Coals.

There are others who, from the Clouds, calculate the Incidents that are to befal them, and see Men on Horseback, Mountains, Ships,
Forests,

Forests, and a thousand other fine Things in the Air; but to see a New Moon the first Time after her Change, on the Right-hand, or directly before you, betokens the utmost good Fortune that Month; as to have her on your Left, or behind you, so that in turning your Head back you happen to see her, foreshews the worst; as also, they say, to be without Gold in your Pocket at that Time, is of very bad Consequence.

I HAVE seen People, who, after writing a Letter, have prognosticated to themselves the ill Success of it, if, by any Accident, it happened to fall on the Ground: Others have seem'd as impatient, and exclaiming against their own Want of Thought, if, thro' Haste or Forgetfulness, they have chanced to hold it before the Fire to dry: But the Mistake of a Word in it, is a sure Omen that whatever Request it carries, shall be refused. Who was the first Inventor of these Forebodings, I know not, but they are now so much the Fashion, especially among the fair Sex, that it is a kind of Rarity to find one free from it.

THERE are, indeed, secret Warnings given, I believe, to all Men, by their better Angels, which ought no more to be neglected, than the Absurdities I have made Mention of, should pass for any thing but what they are, the mere Effects of Chance.

FEW

FEW Men in thefe latter and more corrupted Ages of the World, have Sanctity of Manners, and Piety of Mind, fufficient to entitle them to the Converfation of bleffed Spirits, Face to Face, as did the Patriarchs of old ; and almoft as few who, without that Purity of Soul, have the Gift of *Second Sight*, as it is vulgarly called, but which is no other, in Reality, than the Power of difcerning incorporeal Beings: How, therefore, fhould thofe miniftring Spirits, which the Divine Goodnefs fets over us as Guardians, communicate their Inftructions, excite us to good Actions, deter us from bad ones, or give Notice of the extraordinary Events that fhall befal us, but by intellectual Remonftrances: Something which rifes in the Mind on the fudden, and according to the Will of the fupreme Director of all Things, either dwells in it for a long Time, or fleets away like a Flafh of Lightning, which we neither know whence derived, nor whither fled, but once gone, is no more to be recovered. How often do People fay, *Such a Thing run in their Head?* and tho', according to worldly judging, there was, at that Time, no vifible Reafon for their acting in fuch or fuch a Manner, yet being fway'd by this Impulfe, they could not avoid doing it: Others, again, have cried, *I had once a Thought to go on this or that Expedition, but it went out of my Head.* Thefe are, certainly, the Conferences which the Soul holds, unknown to the Body, with the invifible World, and, I believe, none,

except

except Ideots or Lunaticks, but have experienc'd, more or lefs, of thefe Tranfitions of the Mind.

But as the evil Angels are alfo fometimes permitted to infufe their pernicious Inftincts, it requires both Religion and Penetration to know the one from the other; becaufe thefe Minifters of Darknefs are too fubtil to bid a Man who is not a profeffed Enemy of Virtue, do an Action directly contrary to it; no, they difguife the Poifon they endeavour to inftil, under the Name of a Cordial; they do not directly perfuade to an ill Action, but to fomething which has the Shew of Good, but muft infallibly draw on the contrary. Nor do our Guardian Angels always infpire what is moft pleafing, our Senfes come in for their Part, and will not fuffer the Soul to operate as fhe would do: Hence we liften to fuch Injunctions with Reluctance, and too frequently repel them entirely.

So weak is human Nature, and fo little, while clogg'd with earthly Views, and ever-craving Paffions, are we able to judge rightly of thefe intellectual Admonitions; happy are they who are fo highly favoured, to make a wife Choice; and, I think, there is nothing for which we fhould fo conftantly and earneftly intreat of Heaven, as the Capacity of knowing which of thofe various Suggeftions which we call, and have no other Name for, than *our own Thoughts*, fhould be complied with, and which rejected.

THE

The most plain and remarkable Way, however, by which these Monitors convey their Instructions to us are in Dreams; and tho' some who would be thought very wise, laugh at all who give any Regard to them, yet, I believe, 'tis easy to prove, not only from common Observation, but from Authorities which no-body, who owns the Being of a God, will dare to dispute, that in all Ages of the World, those Men have been looked on as the most Learned and Sagacious, who have known best how to interpret them.

In Sleep the Soul acts apart from the Body; she is released from all those Impediments which confine her Knowledge; and could we, waking, remember, all we have seen in those Interval, I am apt to believe, Futurity would not be so strange to us; but at our Return to Sense, all that is passed dwells but confusedly in the Mind; we can relate but Part, and that too appears so dark, so wrapt up in Clouds, and mingled with other Ideas, that it gives a very faint Resemblance of all those Things which the Soul, I do not doubt, has seen clearly, and without Deception.

Are not the Holy Scriptures full of Examples, how God himself was pleased to reveal himself in Dreams; and I know not, if *Moses* plucking off his Shoes to speak to God in the Bush, was not meant parabolically; for as all

Things are not to be underſtood litterally, eſpecially in that Time when Hierogliphicks were ſo much uſed; I ſee no Reaſon why, by the plucking off his Shoes, might not be meant, that, in Sleep, he threw off all the Paſſions of the Senſes, and had his Soul at Liberty to entertain, and liſten to his great Creator.

Nay, even in the *New Teſtament*, who can judge of St. *Paul*'s being taken into the Third Heaven, any otherwiſe, than that in a Beatifick Viſion, his Soul was preſented with a View of that glorious Place.

'Tis, therefore, methinks, as profane, as it is abſurd, to make a Jeſt, or deſpiſe the Admonitions given us in Sleep; but, even here, as well as in our waking Thoughts, the fallen Angels have Power to tempt and to delude the Imagination: As for Example, if a covetous, and ſordidly avaritious Man dream, that he is ſhewed the Way to a Rich Man's Coffers, and, at his Will, plunders them: Or, if a Man, given up to unlawful Pleaſures, in Sleep, ſatiates his luſtful Appetite in the Embraces of his Neighbour's Wife or Daughter, either of theſe may very well judge ſuch Phantoms ariſe only by the Subtilty of the Devil, who tempts him with an imaginary Poſſeſſion of what he wiſhes, in order to heighten his Deſires, and render him capable of ſticking at nothing, be it never ſo wicked, in order to compaſs his Intent.

Have

HAVE not even, in latter Days, many wonderful Difcoveries been made by Dreams; would not many an Heir, who now lives in the moſt plenteous Manner, have been driven to feek his Bread from Charity, or fome fervile Employment, had not his Birthright been render'd to him by a Dream? Would not many a Murtherer, who, for bathing his Hands in the Heart's Blood of his Fellow-Creature, his Neighbour, his Friend, his Brother, or, perhaps, his Wife, juftly yielded up his Life to the Gallows, be now alive, and triumph in his Crime, believing he had been too fecret in it, even for the Eye of Heaven, had not the deteftable Fact been revealed in a Dream?

AND yet, for all that can be urged, either from Sacred or Profane Hiftory, to give Credit to Dreams, is looked on, as a fit Subject for Ridicule, tho' I do not remember any one Perfon, whether Male or Female, in the whole Courfe of my long and numerous Acquaintance, who has not confeffed, on being ferioufly afked, *That fometime or other, in their Lives, they have had extraordinary Warnings in Dreams, if they would have taken Notice of them.*

ONE, in particular, who, in Publick, feemed to defpife all Regard of Dreams, as favouring too much of Superftition, acknowledged to me, in Private, *That being in great Danger of Ruin,* for the Sum of *Two hundred Pounds*, he had Thoughts of borrowing it of a Relation, who, tho' by many Reasons, under an Obligation of serving him, he knew to be of a Disposition which would not suffer him very readily to comply with his Request: This Humour made the Borrower, who was of a pretty high Spirit, in Debate with himself, as he lay in Bed, if he should chuse Ruin, or an Obligation from so churlish a Person; and he went to Sleep half resolved to run the Hazzard of the former: But his good Angel was kinder to him in this Exigence, than his Unbelief deserved; and he dreamed, that being with his Cousin, he had asked him for the Money, who answered, *That he had not so much at Command, at that Time; but that, he believed, Mr. such a One,* naming a *Person he knew very well, would lend it him, if he would consent to pay a trifling Interest.* As little as he regarded any Admonitions of this Kind, the Dream made so great an Impression on him, that it changed the Intention he had formed before he slept, and early in the Morning, went to seek his Cousin, who repeated to him the very Words he had imagined he heard him speak in his Dream; accordingly, he applied to the Person mentioned, of whom, otherwise, he said, he should not have had the least Thought, and had the Money he desired.

Is it then not strangely ungrateful to the Power which has so far condescended to give us Directions how to proceed, not to acknowledge the

Favours

Favours we receive? Yet are there People, who, after repeated Instances of the Goodness of a directing Providence, have not only denied, but profanely ascribed that to their own Prudence, which could not be foreseen without the immediate Interposition of a Being infinitely superior.

I Knew a Sea-Surgeon, who having been a long Time out of Business, and by that Means reduced to very unhappy Circumstances, was glad, at last, to engage himself, as Surgeon's Mate, with a Master of one of those Ships which go to *Greenland*, on the Whale-Fishery, and, accordingly, had put his Chest of Instruments, Bed, and Cloaths, on Board, and lay, himself, at *Gravesend*, waiting the falling down of the Vessel: Some few Nights before he expected to sail, a venerable Old Man appeared to him in his Sleep, and bad him, *Give over all Thoughts of his Voyage, for the Ship would certainly be lost.* The Dream a little troubled him, but the Remembrance of it soon passed over, till, the second Night, he saw the same Vision again, and the Injunction repeated. This made him begin to think there was something more than ordinary in it, and he could not forbear communicating it to the Head-Surgeon, who lay in the same House with him; but this Man, being too wise, in his own Conceit, to regard Dreams, laughed at his Superstition, and began to repeat several of his own, which seemed remarkable, but nothing

thing, as he said, of Moment happened after them This kind of Discourse again embolden'd him, and, he resolved, in Spite of Omens, to prosecute his Voyage. Well, the third Night, as he lay in Bed, he imagined himself on Board, encompassed with all the Terrors of the Deep, when the Winds and Waves seem to threaten not only those that tempt their Fury, but even those who endeavour to be most secure on Land: He thought the Ship struck, with the utmost Violence, on a Rock, and was staved in a thousand Pieces; that he saw the Master clinging to a Plank, and floating for a Moment, then sunk down beneath a mountainous Billow, which came rushing over him on a sudden: At the same Time Fancy presented him with various dreadful Images of others of the Ship's Crew, perishing in the Storm: The Terror of this Object made him awake with a loud Cry, which was heard by several in the House, who, believing something extraordinary was the Matter, ran hastily into his Chamber, where they found him on his Knees, thanking God he was on Shoar, and solemnly vowing, not to trust himself in a Vessel, which he was now assured would never come Home safe. Nor could all the Persuasions, or Ridicule of those who talked to him on this Head, nor his own Misfortunes, which threatened him with almost starving, prevail with him to undertake this Voyage; but the Wind being fair in a few Hours, he fetched his Things from

from the Ship, and suffered it to depart without him.

The same God who had warned him of the threatened Evil, soon after remedied his Distresses, by raising him a Friend, who recommended him to an *East-India* Captain, with whom he went, and made a safe and profitable Voyage; but, at his Return, enquiring after the *Greenland* Vessel heard it was sunk, and all the Men lost, as he had seen in his Dream, or rather Vision.

To what, then, can we ascribe these Warnings, but to a good Angel; who, while the Faculties of the Body are dead to every Thing, converses with the Soul, and reveals to it as much as the Divine Wisdom thinks fit to permit? Those who are above taking Notice of these intellectual and spiritual Counsels, may imagine themselves Persons of Sagacity, and pass in the World for such, but, doubtless, sometime or other, will repent their Unbelief, and when the Mischief they are bid to avoid, falls on them, will wish, too late, in Bitterness of Heart, that they had been less wise, or, at least, had less affected to be so.

This was the Case of a young Man, who, being of a roving Disposition, would needs quit his Father, whose Darling he was, and go Abroad to see the World, as he called it: He several Times hinted his Inclination, but the old

Man would, by no Means, be brought to consent to it, telling him, *That he was of great Years,
and had now no Comfort of Life, but in his Presence ; besides, as he had no other Person to manage
his Affairs, and was, himself, incapable of doing it,
his Absence would be of the utmost Detriment.* Perceiving, therefore, there was no Hope of parting by Consent, the undutiful Wretch resolved to
go away privately, which wicked Design he accomplished, taking away as much Money and
Plate as he thought would be sufficient to support
him for a considerable Time. The Night after
his Elopement, he dreamed, that he was lying
in a fine Field, the Element above him, the
most serene and beautiful that could be, but,
as he was contemplating, he perceived something
dark over his Head, which turning to examine,
he found it proceeded from a Pair of huge Scales,
that hung, poised by an invisible Hand, in the
Air, but so low, that he feared their falling on him,
and crushing him with their Weight ; a little farther, he beheld, but much higher, a Sword, that
with its Keenness seemed to cut the Clouds which
encompassed it, and at the Point hung Drops of
clotted Blood : Turning his Eyes from so terrible a Prospect, he cast them to the other Side
of the Hemisphere, which presented itself to
him full of innumerable Circles that were cut
cross and cross by other Lines, and from the
Middle of each, long Darts shot forth, with all
their Points levelled at him : He told me, *That
in a frosty Night the Sky is not more spangled with
Stars,*

Stars, than in his Dream it appeared with Circles. He awoke much terrified, but, as many others do, thought it childish, or foolish, to regard any Occurrences which should befal in Sleep.

In short, he went on his intended Progress, but had not proceeded far, before he met with Robbers, who took from him all the Money and Bills he had about him, and being obliged to beg his Way to the Place where he expected a Recruit, having left the Plate he took from his Father, in the Hands of a wild Companion of his, who was to dispose of it, and remit the Money by the Post; but having waited a considerable Time, and no Letter arriving, he wrote to an Acquaintance, to enquire after this unfaithful Steward, who sent him the melancholly Account, That he was gone to the *Indies*. Having lived on Credit, and now without Means to discharge the Obligations he had contracted, he was thrown into Prison, whence he had no Hope of being relieved, but by the Goodness of a forgiving Father, to whom he, therefore, wrote, acknowledging his Fault, like the Prodigal in Scripture, and begging to be again received: But his Penitence, if real, came too late; the old Man had paid the Debt of Nature, declaring, with his last Words, *That the Disobedience and Wickedness of his Son had broke his Heart*. Nobody who had any Regard to the Heir being present, his Effects were, in a Manner, cast Lots for,

for, every one getting a Part, but him who had the sole Right to the Whole.

THE poor Prisoner, therefore, remained so, without Relief, without Hope, without Sustenance, but what he received from the Hands of common Charity; and to these Calamities, a greater still added, which was the Reflection that all this had fallen on him, entirely thro' his own Obstinacy.

HAVING lingered many Months in this miserable Condition, he was, at length, set at Liberty, thro' the Compassion of his Creditors, on his Promise, *That, if ever able, he would pay.* He then came to *London,* almost naked and famished; he entreated some small Succour from those who possessed what he ought to have been Master of, but was refused it with opprobrious Language, well-knowing it was not in his Power to compel them to do him Justice. Having been well educated, he, in time, found Means to write for Lawyers, and thereby sustained a Life full of Hardships, but such ill Fate still attended him, that whatever he got, he was always defrauded of. He set up a little School, and taught Boys to read, write, and understand the Grammar, by which he might have lived tolerably handsome, had he not been compelled to leave it, on a Bastard Child being laid to him: In fine, he was no sooner settled in any Business he took in Hand, but, by some Accident

Accident or other, he was obliged to quit it. Twenty Years had paſſed over with him in this Manner, ſtill ſtruggling againſt the Stream, always labouring, but always diſappointed, and evermore miſerable, and in Debt: When I firſt happened into his Acquaintance, he ſeemed pleaſed with me, and, after relating to me the various Misfortunes he had gone thro', told me alſo his Dream, as I have before recited it. On which I told him, *That, without being guilty of Flattery, I could not promiſe he would ever ſee a good Day in this World; for the Scales hanging over his Head, plainly betokened his Fate was that Moment in the Balance; that he had done what merited the ſevereſt Puniſhment, and the Sword of Juſtice, which he ſaw behind him, was unſheathed to execute it: Thoſe Circles, with their Darts pointed to him, as far as he could ſee in the Element, were the Years he ſhould number in Life, which ſhould all come armed with Calamities and Heart-diſtracting Grief.*

He aſſured me, *That nothing was more certain than the Interpretation I had given; that he had already proved the Truth of it: and expected, indeed, no End of his Vexations till Death.*

I have not ſeen him ſome Years, but, if he be living, I dare anſwer, he is ſtill in the ſame Condition as when he made this Complaint.

I could bring many Examples to prove that Dreams are not merely the Effect of a disturbed Imagination, but real Warnings or Excitements, sometimes of a good, sometimes of a bad Angel; but these will be sufficient to an understanding Reader.

These I have named may very justly be called *Omens*, and are, indeed, the only ones that can be depended on: Not but I have some little Faith in the Howling of a Dog, when it does not proceed from Hunger, Blows or Confinement. As odd and unaccountable as it may seem, those Animals scent Death, even before it seizes a Person. An intimate Friend of mine, for some Days before he was taken with his last Sickness, could never sit down in the Park, or in a Field, without having a Dog throw up the Earth, and make a Hole close by him, in the Form of a Grave. A strange Dog was heard to howl very terribly, without any visible Cause, for several Nights together, preceeding that in which a Neighbour of mine departed this Life: Nor is the Croaking of a Raven, or the Chirping of a Cricket, to be wholly disregarded, as little as they are consonant to Reason, tho', as I said before, I would not have any-body look on them as infallible Prognosticks.

CHAP.

CHAP. VII.

On Predestination.

THERE are two Things to which, we may depend on, we are pre-ordained before we ever see Light, which is the Time and Manner of our Death, and Marriage, if fated ever to enter into that State: The First it is certain that we must all come to, but the Latter many People avoid. As to other Incidents, they are greatly left to our own Choice; and nothing can be more absurd, than for People, after having drawn on themselves, by their own Imprudence, some very great Misfortune, cry, *'Twas their Fate, and they could not withstand it.* It seems to me, that those Persons, be they of what Religion they will, who support the Doctrine of Predestination in all Events, are no better than Blasphemers of the Divine Goodness; Is it agreeable to Infinite Justice and Mercy to pre-ordain, which is only another Word for compelling a Person to Vices, for which he merits eternal Punishments? For what is Reason, the distinguishing Power, given us, but to pursue Good, and fly from Evil? If, in spite of that Knowledge, we

are obliged to make Choice of that which is abhorred by Heaven, and muſt bring Diſtruction on ourſelves? I know, very well, that what St. *Paul* ſays, in the viith, viiith, and ixth Chapters of his Epiſtle to the *Romans*, is the Ground-Work on which the Aſſerters of Predeſtination have built their Scheme, but they ſeem, methinks, to forget, that St. *Paul*, who was a very learned Man, did not write to every Capacity; and as they, with ſo much Earneſtneſs, quote thoſe particular Verſes, which they imagine favour the Tenets they think fit to hold, they ought not to leave neglected this Sentence of the ſame Author, *Shall we make God the Author of Evil then? No, God forbid.* Nothing can be more plain, than that he is ſo, if he lays us under an abſolute Neceſſity of Sinning: but to leave theſe Things to the Divines, it is equally as unhappy to be under the Direction of a Supreme Power, who creates us for no other Purpoſe than to be wretched: I am certain, therefore, it is much more conſonant to Religion, and the Idea we have of God, to acknowledge the Calamities we ſuſtain, wholly owing to ourſelves, either by a too violent Purſuit in the Gratification of our Paſſions, or our Inadvertency, and Careleſneſs in the Purſuit of our Advantage: And, I would fain have any one of thoſe Millions, who daily exclaim on their ill Fortune, ſeriouſly examine their own Conduct, and then give their impartial Judgment; I dare anſwer, that there is none but will confeſs, they might have avoided their

Misfortunes,

Misfortunes, if they had considered as well before, as afterwards.

As to the Period of Time we are to stay in this World, as I said before, it certainly is fixed, nor can all our Endeavours retard it, even for a Moment: And, as to that of Marriage, I am much of the same Mind; because I have known Men who have lived Batchelors till their Decline, and, at last, contrary to the Opinion of all the World, and even of themselves, have married. You'll say, perhaps, *It was because they never before met with a Woman whom they could like*, or, *was an agreeable Match*: No, I have been acquainted with Persons who have loved, been beloved, nothing wanting but the Ceremony, yet have broke off by Accidents the most unaccountable in the World, and without any Falshood on either Side, yet have both Parties, afterwards, married others on the sudden; and where, oftentimes, there has been as little Prospect of Felicity, as there was of a great deal, had they been united in Youth to those where Affection and Merit at first engaged them.

These, therefore, I am positive, have their certain Times allotted, and it is not in our Power, either to anticipate, or delay them, a Moment; but, as for other Events, they depend entirely on ourselves, and according as Reason is strong or weak in us, we act either for our good or ill Fortune. How happens it then, may some alledge,

ledge, that we frequently see the best concerted Schemes fail of their Design, while the Measures taken by others, succeed, even beyond Expectation? To which I answer, That the same Measures, prosecuted in the same Manner, and at the same Time, would certainly produce the same Effect with one Man as with another: But here it is that the Planets may justly be said to have a great Share in the Incidents of humane Life: One Man shall happen to undertake his Enterprize in an Hour when the benificent Planets shed their Influence; another shall go about it when the Malignant ones are in Force: and to this, in great Measure, we may impute the Difference of their Success. For the Benefit of my Readers, I will, therefore, give them a Detail of the lucky and unlucky Hours.

The Prosperous are those under the Direction of

  The *Sun* ☉,
  Jupiter ♃,
  Venus ♀,
  Mercury ☿,

The Malevolent ones are those under,

  Saturn ♄,
  Mars ♂.

In some Affairs the Hour of the *Moon* may be Favourable, but it is only when your Business is with People of a low Rank; she otherwise
          promises

promises you little, but deceitful Hopes. You ought, however, to be extremely careful in observing her Degrees, for so great is her Influence, that tho' you should attempt any thing under the most fortunate Aspect, her Decline will blast it all. But having said thus much, it is in every one's Power to chuse a lucky Hour, only by regarding heedfully *Parker's Ephemeris*.

Those invisible Warnings which we receive from our good Angel, as mentioned in the foregoing Chapter, concerning Omens, ought also to be observed with the utmost Care. It is, but with great Pains and Labour, we Mortals find out the Method of chusing a propitious Moment; but these Spirits, who, at once, comprehend whatever is done in the World, and see into the most hidden Causes, fail not to give Notice to the Souls committed to their Charge, when it is we ought, or ought not, to venture on any great Enterprize.

It is very much to this, many People, whose good Fortune amazes us, are indebted, for not being as Unhappy as they are Prosperous.

There are also other superior Means by which some have raised to themselves great Fortunes, the Cheif of which is *Magic*, vulgarly called the *Black Art*; which, indeed, is no other than the Knowledge of certain Spells, by which you may attain a kind of Authority over one of

G the

the invisible World, and compel a Spirit so rais'd, to reveal whatever you are desirous of knowing: Nor is this to be done by Witchcraft, or making a Contract with the Devil, as some are so silly to imagine, but by the understanding some Cabalistical Words, Characters, and Figures, made Use of in a proper Time and Place: The next are those *Talismans* of which I have already treated. The wearing of a Loadstone may very well come in for a third Place in the Mystic Roll of secret *Recipes*, to procure Ease for all the Calamities to which Life is incident. But, as the Virtues of this admirable Stone deserve a particular Description, I shall treat of it hereafter, in a Chapter by itself, and return to my first Design in this.

PREDESTINATION, therefore, whatever some great Men may have said in the Defence of it, was, at first, no more than an Invention found out to lay the Blame of our own ill Conduct on the Compulsion of an inevitable Fate: Believe me, who, tho' I pretend not to any Share of Learning, have, from my Childhood, not only been blessed with a perfect Knowledge of Nature, but likewise of Things and Beings supernatural, that we cannot put a more gross Deception on ourselves, than to listen to the Doctrine of it.

BESIDES, it seems to me not only a false, but an impolitick Supposition also; it is, in the first Place,

Place, an Enemy to Religion; for, if regarded in Matters of Salvation, what Occasion have we to offer up Sacrifice and Prayer? What Need of good Works, or what Danger of ill Ones, if Predestination cuts off all Reward for the one, or Punishment for the other? How can the Maintainers of this Tenet answer their manifest Contradiction of the Text, *Every Man shall be judged according to his Works*, if, before we are capable of any Works, we are doomed to everlasting Happiness, or Misery? Must it not make the best Christian very faint and languid in his Devotions, when he considers that he stands no better a Chance to be an Inheritor of the Kingdom of Heaven, than the most Profligate of his Neighbours? And, must it not make the Libertine more bold in Wickedness, to be assured, his Sins will not add to his Damnation?

Then, if considered, in Regard of our being happy in this Life, nothing can be more opposite: It is the utter Destruction of all the Social Virtues; to what End do we aim at Learning, endeavour to be well-bred, accomplished, and good-natur'd, but to be agreeable to those we are to pass our Time with? If predestined to the Fate of being beloved, admired, applauded, we may be as churlish as we please, and save ourselves a vast Expence of Pains and Money too. There would be none of that laudable Emulation which excites to vye with our Neighbours in all that is Praise-worthy: No Man would give himself the Trouble of correcting the Faults in his Nature, or endeavour to improve the Beauties of it, but all would be wild and savage, and we should differ from the Brute-Creation in nothing but in Form.

But, as it is needless to urge any thing against so pernicious a Doctrine, to those who condemn it, so it will be altogether as vain to preach to those who have their own Reasons to support it; but if I may be allowed to speak my Mind, I believe few do it who have any Regard to any thing, either here or hereafter.

CHAP. VIII.

On the POWER of SYMPATHY.

THO' I know this is a Subject which has been already frequently treated on by Pens infinitely more capable of doing Justice to it, than mine can pretend to, yet, because these Tracts are, most of them, too voluminous, as well as too abstruse for the Perusal of the Generality of my fair Readers, I shall oblige them with some Hints, which, perhaps, may be of Service to them.

THE

The Word Sympathy means no other than a certain Bent, or inclining of one Thing to another; and that there is such an Inclination, Nature declares visible in all her Works, as well inanimate as animate: Nothing can be more wonderful than that Sympathy of the *Palm Trees*, which, being planted at some Distance from each other, shoot forth their Branches, all on one Side, till they meet, and mingle: It has, also, been observed of these Trees, that if one be cut down, the other bows its Head, and soon withers away.

The Steel and Loadstone are known and plain Truths of Sympathy; and tho' there are People who strenuously deny some of the Effects imputed to it, yet all agree to acknowledge this.

The Sympathy between the different Sexes of animated Beings, even in the Brute Creation, may, every Day, be seen long before the least Desire of Copulation warms the Blood: A Male and Female Kitten will agree together much better than two of the same Kind; young Pidgeons will do the same, and, in fine, every Thing that has Life finds a Tendency in itself; which is no other Way to be accounted for, than by the Power of Sympathy.

These Things, therefore, being paſt Diſpute, I ſhall leave them, and proceed to others which have furniſhed the learned World with ſo much Matter for Argument.

The Sympathetic Powder, ſo much talked of for the wondrous Cures it has performed, by being applied to the Weapon which gave the Wound, has occaſioned great Debates, but, I perceive, the moſt learned of our Phyſicians have given their Opinion in Favour of it, and that, in general, it is more believed than practiſed.

Why, therefore, ſhould it ſeem ſo ſtrange, that the wearing certain Amulets, or Charms, ſhould excite the Paſſion of Love in a Perſon whoſe Name is thereon written, or engraved? Nothing is more true, than that this is Fact; but, becauſe all the Arguments in the World fall ſhort of Proof, I will demonſtrate it in a little Hiſtory which, not only myſelf, but all my Family, can aver.

A young Woman, of a good Family, and well educated, but without any Fortune, or the Hope of any, being maintained by her Godmother, the All of whoſe Subſtance conſiſted in Annuities, and, conſequently, would have nothing to bequeath at her Deceaſe, happened to fall, accidentally, in Company with a Gentleman

of

of a moſt accompliſhed Perſon, and great Eſtate: His Merits had an Effect on her, common in a youthful Heart, and now ſhe began to lament that Poverty which could not ſuffer her to entertain any Expectation of being as agreeable in his Eyes, as he had been in hers. She frequently ſaw him at the Houſe of an Acquaintance, where they both viſited, and every Time became more enamoured, and more melancholly, than before. An old Woman, with whom ſhe was very intimate, obſerved a Change in her Countenance and Behaviour, and never left off importuning her, till ſhe was Miſtreſs of the Secret; which, as ſoon as ſhe was, ſhe perſuaded her to divulge, and that ſhe would go with her to a Perſon, whoſe Skill in Affairs of that Nature, ſhe aſſured her, ſhe had formerly experienced, bidding her be of good Heart; for, if the Gentleman were not already married, ſhe would warrant this Philoſopher would contrive it ſo, that ſhe ſhould be his Bride. People in Love are ready enough to flatter themſelves with the leaſt Shadow that ſeems to promiſe them Succeſs, and half her Griefs were diſſipated before ſhe came to the Houſe of the Perſon who was to preſcribe the Means of her Cure.

Having related her Caſe, and given the accuſtomed Fee, which, I think, ſhe told me was Two Guineas, with a promiſary Note of Fifty Pounds when ſhe ſhould be the Wife of ſuch a Gentleman; he made her be let Blood before him, in the Foot, and ſaving, carefully, the

Blood, bid her come to him on the third Day; it is not to be boubted but she was punctual, and he then delivered to her a small Cake, but made extreamly rich with Sweatmeats in one Part of it, on which he made a Mark; he told her, *There was something that should render the Person that should eat it, incapable of being easy out of her Company:* As for the rest, he said, *she might give it to whom she pleased, for there was nothing in it, either of Good or Harm*: But several Times repeated his Charge, *That she would take Care nobody should taste of the other, but the Gentleman she desired to engage.*

WHEN she gave me this Account, she told me, she was in the utmost Perplexity to get this Injunction fulfilled, having gone several Times to the House of her Acquaintance, without finding the Gentleman, but she still kept the Cake in her Pocket, wrapped in a Piece of clean Paper, and, at last, being so lucky to meet him, took it out, and calling for a Knife, told them, she would let them taste a Rarity; having divided it into small Slices, she took Care to serve every-body before him, that he might not chuse the wrong Piece; in fine, she had the Satisfaction to see him swallow it all, and soon after took her Leave, having been ordered by the Sage so to do, and went to him for further Advice how to proceed: On which, he gave her something sewed up in green Silk, which he bid her wear continually in her Bosom, next her Flesh, and

and take the utmost Care not to lose it, or suffer it to be opened, either by herself, or any other Person. This, he assured her, would not only oblige the Man desired to marry her, but also to be the most fond Husband in the World, as long as he lived.

But, not to spin out my Narration, she soon found the Effects of what had been done; the Gentleman became infinitely in Love with her, courted, and in a few Weeks, was married to her, nor did Enjoyment, in the least, damp the Fervour of his Passion; for four Years it seemed rather, every Day, to increase; insomuch, that he studied nothing but how to prove his Affection; he did nothing without consulting her; her Will was his Law in every thing; all for whom she had a Kindness, were sure of his Esteem; and whoever she disliked, were looked upon as his Enemies. Never was a happier Woman, while she obeyed the Directions abovementioned; but, being one Day alone, and contemplating the good Fortune to which she was arrived, and the Means of it, the Curiosity of her Sex tempted her to peep into the green Silk Bag, so that unripping one Corner of it; she saw a small Quantity of a whitish Substance, but more like Smoak than Powder, issue from it, and fly away, beyond all Possibility of catching it again; she was a little frighted to find any of it gone, but comforted herself with the Belief, that she was too well established in her Husband's
Af-

Affections, to lose it, after so long a Time, and that, if it should be so, she could go again to the Philosopher, to recruit her Bag.

But sadly did she find herself deceived, when her Husband coming Home, accosted her not as he was accustomed to do, with open Arms, and all the fond Expressions that the violent Passion could suggest, but with a sullen and dejected Air, that, instead of flying to her Bosom, and warming it with a thousand Sighs of Tenderness, he returned not the Salute she gave him, but flung from her, as from a Creature he either hated, or despised, and whose Touch was loathsome.

She now perceived the Misfortune she had brought upon herself, but endeavoured to bring him into Humour, and intreated he would let her know what she had done to offend him? to which he refused making any Answer, for a long Time, but being pressed by her Importunities, he, at last, told her, *That he had been considering the Injury he had done his Family, by marrying a Woman without a Fortune, and, that if it was to do again, he would as soon be damned; that he wondered what he had seen in her to bewitch him, for, that there were a thousand finer Women, with good Portions, he might have had his Choice, and that he could not forgive himself, nor should ever be easy more.* These, and many more Speeches of the like rude and unkind Nature, were her Entertaintainment all that Night; but, thinking to retrieve all yet, she arose early in the Morning, and went in Search of him who had given her the Charm, and, to her great Mortification, was told, he had been dead a Month. She now looked on her Misery as irremediable, and grew as disconsolate as her Husband ill-natured. They lived in the most discontented Manner imaginable, but her Condition was infinitely the worst, because, now resuming the Care of his own Purse, he found Means to indulge himself Abroad, with those Pleasures he could no longer find at Home; while she, the most abandoned, and most wretched Creature in the World, had no more Allowance from him, than was just sufficient to sustain Nature.

IN this unhappy Situation she had Recourse to me, having heard I had performed some very extraordinary Things that Way; she related to me the whole History of the Affair, from the Beginning to the End, concluding with telling me, *That tho' her Husband's Parsimony at present, gave her not the Power of making me any Present, yet, if I could be able, once more, to recover his Affection for her, she should then have enough to give.* But I would not deceive her: I told her, it was not in *Nature*, or in *Art*, to recal a Passion which owed its Original to *Compulsion*; I confess'd, that a Desire which arose by *Nature*, if grown cool, might be revigorated by *Art*, but as his to her, had been only the Effects of *Art*, and was a
Force

Force on his Faculties, all second Endeavours would be ineffectual to bring it back.

She found my Words but too true, and tho', as I afterwards heard, she had Recourse to others, who dealt with less Sincerity than I had done, yet did all the Expectations they had raised in her, prove abortive, and she lived and died a miserable, and, by all who heard what she had done, as, at last, she was foolish enough to reveal it, a most unpitied and despised Woman.

The *French* and *Italians*, have many Secrets to excite Love, or rather Desire; for, I think, a Passion which owes not its Being to Nature, unassisted by Art of any Kind, cannot, justly, be termed Love; but I would have all, to whom I wish well, be careful how they make Use of any such Prescriptions, lest, ignorant of what they do, they prejudice the Person they aim to engage. I knew a Woman, who being desirous a certain Gentleman of my Acquaintance should make his Addresses to her, applied to one of these Dealers in the Trade of forcing Inclination, who ordered her to put a Paper of Powder, which he gave her, into some kind of Liquor that the Gentleman should drink: Accordingly she put it into Punch, of which, when he had drank plentifully, he found himself seized with Desires more violent than he had ever before experienced, he was even mad; and, tho' the least Thought of Love had never entered into his

his Head for this Woman, yet was he now so overborn with a wild Inclination for the Enjoyment of her, that being alone with her, it was as much as she could do, to hinder him from committing a Rape; but, as Marriage was the Thing she aimed at, she proposed it to him, telling him, *That since he had so great a Passion for her, she was ready to consent on lawful Terms:* But this failing, not but that he would have done any thing in those distracted Moments, to have possessed her; but it being too late in the Night to procure a Clergyman, she was obliged to call the People of the House to her Assistance, and, by their Means, put him into a Chair, and sent him Home: Seeing the Powder had wrought this Effect, she doubted not, in the least, but he would be at her Lodgings early in the Morning, and accomplish what she intended by giving him this Dose; but she was infinitely mistaken, the Powder, which had so much inflamed him, being no other than *Cantharides*, threw out its Venom in a violent Rash, all over his Body, and left his Heart cool as before he had taken it; but remembering the Vehemence of his Desires the Night before, it appeared extremely strange to him, and relating the whole Affair, both to myself, and an eminent Physician, I presently gave my Opinion, that something had been given him to cause those extraordinary Emotions, on which, the Doctor said, it was *Cantharides*. The Gentleman was so much enraged to find he had been practised on in such a Manner, that he resolved,

solved, whatever it cost him, to know the Truth, and, in fine, partly by Persuasions, and partly by Bribes, he discovered where she had been that Day; which he had no sooner done, than he threatened the old Fellow who had given her the Powder, in so terrible a Manner, that he fell on his Knees, and related the whole Affair, on Promise of Forgiveness.

THE Sequel of this Business was, that the Gentleman who had before a good Regard, as far as Friendship, for that Woman, now became her implacable Enemy, and could not think on her, without the utmost Loathing and Detestation.

THESE Things are both dangerous and pernicious, and, in my Opinion, will not be made Use on, but by People abandoned in their Principles and Characters; but as to the wearing *Sigils*, or *Amulets*, which are only to create a general good Will and Esteem, I see no Reason, either in Religion or Morality, to disapprove them.

THOSE People who most despise the Use of them, cannot, without being very unjust, alledge, that there is any Hurt in having them about you, either to yourself, or any other Person: The Characters of the *one* being made on consecrated Parchment, and the Composition of the *other*, such Things as are frequently taken
in-

inwardly to comfort and corroborate the Vital Faculties, such as Corral, Ambergrease, &c. and not the least Mixture of any thing that is diabolical, either in the Ingredients, or Words, tho' wrote in Figures unintelligible to all but those of the Cabal.

But in spite of all that has, or can be said to the contrary, I positively maintain, from a long Experience, both in myself, and those that have given them, that they not only attract the Goodwill of others, but excite also in the Person who wears them, a Propensity to do those Actions which merit Praise and Love.

In fine, they are an inferior Sort of *Talismans*, working, in a meaner Degree, the same Effects; and tho' they cannot be said to change Fate, rendering one who is very wretched, happy in an Instant, yet they serve to soften the Severity of it; and, tho' a Person may be miserable, with one of them about him, yet would he be much more so, should he leave them off, as has been tried by some, into whose Hands, it is possible, this Book may fall, and have, afterwards, confessed to me how dearly they have repented the Experiment.

It is certain, I have known People, who, on first putting them on, have fancied to themselves Things which I never promised, nor are in the Power of Art to perform; tho' working in

a Gara Garret, or a Cellar, they have expected no less than keeping a Coach and Six, forgetting, that no Person is reasonably to depend on more than being fortunate in the Business to which he has been allotted, either by the Choice of his Parents, or his own Inclination; and, I think, if these *Sigils*, or *Amulets*, are of Force to make him so, he ought to be very well content.

YET, so much does Ambition swell the meanest Soul, that not one but would be glad to fill the Post of the first Minister of State; nay, and imagine themselves fit for it too: I have known a Cobler, in his Stall, pretend to regulate the whole Affairs of *Europe*, and give Laws to all the Monarchs in the World.

HENCE it follows, that not only *Sigils*, and *Amulets*, but even *Talismans*, sometimes, fail of their Effect; for, not being able to work Miracles, the real good Fortune they bring, is slighted, and they are plucked out, and, perhaps, thrown away, before they have fulfilled half, what a little more, even, sometimes, the smallest Point of Time, would have brought to Perfection.

BUT, as it is only the Ignorant that can be guilty of such Follies, I leave them to the Correction of their own Impatience and Stupidity, which will not fail doing it in a severer Manner than I wish. Those of the wiser Sort, who either

ther have bought of me, or shall hereafter buy of my Wife, any of these prevailing Charms, whether *Talisman*, *Sigil*, or *Amulet*, will, I doubt not, be satisfied with the Purchase, and reap all the Benefits which can be expected from it.

CHAP. IX.

On the Difference between NATURAL *and* DIABOLICAL MAGIC.

AVING in some former Chapters had Occasion to mention this Art in its two Branches, I think it highly necessary to explain what it is I mean by this Distinction.

I KNOW the Vulgar are apt to look on every thing which they cannot comprehend, as brought about by the Assistance of the Devil, and this they call the *Black-Art*, but is known, among the learned World, by the Name of *Necromancy*: How far this Study, or the Practice of it, is, or is not, condemnable, I will not pretend to determine, all that I shall concern myself about it, shall be, to set forth how vastly distant it is from *Magic Simple*, and *Natural*: The one teaches how to raise Infernal Spirits by the Help of certain Words and
Spells,

Spells, the other, only how to make a proper Ufe of thofe Things which are common to us, and for which we need ranfack no other World than this we are born and live in; and, that the Knowledge of this is fo far from being criminal, that it is not only laudable, but highly neceffary alfo, for all fuch as take upon them to give Inftructions for the Conduct of others, in the Affairs of Life: Neither ought Phyficians, or Surgeons, to be ignorant of it, as has been already proved in the foregoing Difcourfe on the Power of Sympathy.

GREAT is the Power of certain Herbs, if gathered under the Influence of proper Planets, and greater yet is that of Minerals, provided the Afpect for digging, and applying them, be rightly underftood: What Bufinefs has the Devil or his Agents with this? Is it a Fault to know the Virtues of Things created for our Ufe; or can that Science be guilty, which informs us when, and in what Manner, to prepare them fo as to be beneficial to Mankind.

IT cannot, indeed, be denied, but that there are Plants and Minerals which may be made Ufe of to the Prejudice of our Neighbours, and that the fame Science teaches the Means of both a good and an evil Application; but what of that? muft we, becaufe we know how to do a Mifchief, be guilty of it? Muft we needs try Practices upon our Fellow-Creatures? No certainly:

tainly: And we might as well forbid a Student in Phyſick to conſider the Effects of Poiſon, for fear, knowing how to give it, he ſhould adminiſter it inſtead of a wholeſome *Recipe*. Can any thing be more abſurd than this Way of arguing? Yet ſome, who are accounted great Men, make Uſe of it.

CHYMISTRY, if truly underſtood, comes the neareſt to *Natural Magic* of any Science in the World; yet the Study of it is ſo far from being blameable, that thoſe who have attained to any Degree of Perfection therein, have always been looked on as extraordinary Perſons: What can be more wonderful, than the Power it gives to tranſmute Metals, and change the very Nature of Things, rendering the moſt hard and rocky Subſtances ſoft and maleable, and converting the ſpungy into indiſſoluble?

ASTRONOMY alſo bears a Part with *Chymiſtry*, in an Affinity with *Natural Magic*, and whoever is perfectly verſed in thoſe two Sciences, wants but a very little of comprehending the whole Myſtery of the other: Neither of them alone, indeed, can do any great Matter towards it, but when both are joined, eſpecially if aſſiſted by that Part of the Mathematicks which teaches Number and Proportion, that Knowledge may effect moſt of thoſe Wonders which are commonly attributed to *Magic*.

NATURAL MAGIC, therefore, is, in reality, no more than the Perfection of *Philofophy*, which, certainly, no Man in his right Wits, but would be proud to have the Capacity of attaining.

IT is certain, that the little Skill I have in this Science, has drawn Afperfions on me of different Kinds; the Ignorant perceiving what was in my Power to bring about, have cried out, I dealed with the Devil; and the more learned have faid, I was an Impoftor: The former not being able to comprehend how the Effects I wrought could proceed from Caufes merely Natural; and the latter, fenfible of the Difficulties which attend an Inquifition into thofe occult Studies, could not believe, a Perfon who never was bleffed with the Ufe of Speech, or Hearing, and, therefore, denied many Advantages, which muft neceffarily arife from thofe two Senfes, fhould acquire an Underftanding in fuch dark and abftrufe Myfteries, which very few of the moft deeply learned could fathom.

THUS have I fuffered on the one Hand, for being fufpected to know too much, and, on the other, as a Man who pretended to know more than he did; but, as I take Heaven to witnefs, that I never, in my whole Life, had Recourfe to diabolic Means, fo I, alfo, never deceived thofe who confulted me, by endeavouring to pafs on them for a greater Man than I am.

I SHALL

I SHALL not be so vain, to say, the Secrets I am Master of, have been the Acquisition of my own Labour; no, I have neither Learning, nor Reading enough, by the thousandth Part, for it, but I have been favoured with them by Persons who have spent the greatest Part of their Lives in this Study. I never can sufficiently make known the Obligations I have to a *Hebrew Rabbi*, before-mentioned, on the Account of the *Talismans*; yet am I still infinitely more indebted to a *Chinese*, who, having gone thro' all the Learning his native Country could afford, ranged three Parts of the Globe in Search of more, and about some nine Years since, passed thro' this Island in his Tour.

ANOTHER very venerable Man, from whom I learned many curious Things, was an *Assyrian*, of the *Grecian* Church: He loved me with a kind of Paternal Affection, and told me, *If I would accompany him to his Country, he would make me be looked upon, among them, as a Person sent from Heaven to do Good.* The Ingratitude I have since met with, has made me frequently, when I have reflected on it, regret that I followed not his Advice; but, as I am satisfied it is the Will of the supreme Disposer of all Things, I endure it, resigned, and, as much as the Passions of frail, humane Nature will permit, contented also.

But, say those who are Enemies to *Magic* of all Kinds, *It teaches the Means of conversing with Spirits, and that is unlawful and unwarrantable among Christians*. Before an Answer be made to such an Objection, they ought to bring some Proof from Holy Writ why it is unwarrantable, which, I believe, they would be greatly at a Loss to do. But, however, for the Satisfaction of my Readers, I will confess all they can alledge as to this Matter of Fact; 'tis true, there are Means, and very innocent ones too, of rendering visible some Beings which none but those of the Cabal have any Notion of; but, if these Beings are so far from being ill, that they are infinitely purer than the most elevated Sort, while cased in Flesh, can pretend to be, it cannot be denied, but our Conversation with them will be far from a Disadvantage to us; and, I think, it must be also owned, that the Knowledge of such a Secret can do us no Harm, tho' we should refrain making Use of it in this Branch, viz. *Holding Intelligence with Aerial Spirits*.

All that I attempt to prove, is, that *Natural Magic* has nothing in it repugnant to the Laws of God; and, as for Man, it would certainly be the better for the World if there were many who studied it.

The Vanity of latter Times, makes Men imagine they are wiser, and more learned,
than

than their Fore-fathers, and that every Age adds some new Improvement in the Sciences; whereas, on the contrary, we grow darker and darker, and, like *Martha* in the *New Testament*, busy ourselves about Trifles, and leave the most essential Study, which, next to Religion, I still say is *natural Magic*, wholly neglected and uncultivated.

CHAP. X.

On APPARITIONS.

KNOW nothing more feared, and at the same Time, less believed than Apparitions: Those who argue the most strenuously against them, and affect most to ridicule all Accounts given of them, are frequently, on finding themselves in the Dark, as much terrified, meerly by the Strength of their own Imagination, as the Persons who give the greatest Credit to them.

A MERRY Instance of this kind happened about twenty Years ago: Some Gentlemen being drinking at the *Bell* Tavern in *Westminster*, the Conversation fell accidentally on Apparitions; as they were of different Opinions, the Dispute grew high; but one among them, being willing to be thought more Courageous than the rest, and to testify how little he believed any such Stories, offered to go alone into the Abbey at Twelve o' Clock at Night, and down into the Royal Vault within King *Henry* the Seventh's Chapel, which happened then to be open on account of some Person of Quality who was to be buried there the next Day. Those who were of the other Party, laid twenty Guineas he durst not perform his Promise; but he accepted the Wager, and Mr. *West* the Verger was sent for, to whom they gave a Crown for his Trouble of opening the Doors. The Hour appointed being arrived, all the Company conducted the bold Adventurer to the Church-yard, and one of them asking him, *How they should know he went so far as he pretended*, he made Answer, *That he would stick his Penknife into the Earth within the Vault, which, after his Return, they might go into, accompanied by the Verger, with a Light, and find there.* Every Thing being thus agreed, the Gate was opened, and he admitted, the Gentlemen tarrying with Mr. *West* till he should come out; but he staying considerably longer than was expected, they all (especially those of them who believed Spirits) imagined something had happened to punish his Temerity; on which it was concluded to enter in Search of him. The venerable Look of that ancient Pile, the hollow Murmurs the Wind made through the Arches of the adjacent Cloysters, and the

Eccho

Eccho which, in the Stilness of the Night, repeated every Foot-step, together with the Reflection of the Number of Dead they passed over, gave the whole Company such Ideas, as made the most courageous amongst them to confess, he would not be there alone, and in the Dark, for a much greater Wager than had been stak'd. At length they arrived at the Vault, where, as soon as they descended the first Stair, they beheld their Companion lying Motionless at the Bottom. On endeavouring to raise him, they perceived he had stuck his Penknife through the right Skirt of his Coat. It was with great Difficulty they recovered him from his Swoon; and when he was so, could get little from him, till after they re-conducted him to the Tavern; when being a little refreshed, they desired he would tell them what had happened to occasion the Disorder they found him in: On which he broke into the utmost Exclamations against all those who disbelieved Spirits, and said, *That he had been guilty of the utmost Presumption, and that he was now convinced of his Error*: But they repeating their former Request, he confess'd, "*That the Door was no sooner closed upon him, than he was seized with Apprehensions which made him repent his Boldness, and more than once prompted him to go back; but the Fear of being laughed at overcame his other Terrors, insomuch, that he proceeded to the Vault, where every Thing that was shocking to Nature encreased on him, yet still the Pride of performing what he had so confidently pretended to,*

remaining,

remaining, he went down the Stairs, and when he came to the last, stooped to stick his Penknife in the Earth, thinking it sufficient for the winning of the Wager that he left it within the Vault, it not being specified in the Agreement, how far he should go into it: but, said he, *as I was in this Action, I felt something pluck me by the Coat, which prevented my rising, and with the instant Horror threw me into the Condition you saw.* He had no sooner concluded his little Account, than the whole Company set up a loud Laugh, which strangely surprising him, they shewed him the Penknife, which was still hanging in the Skirt of his Coat, and convinced him, that in the Hurry of Stooping, he had stuck it thro, which Detainment, weak as it was, with the Confusion of his Thoughts, had made him imagine something Supernatural.

THOUGH this Gentleman neither saw, heard, or felt any Thing in reality, yet the unusual Dread he had on him at this Juncture, may prove that there is an innate Apprehension, even in the boldest Minds, on the Score of Apparitions. The Shadows which frequently the Moon makes with the moving of a Bough, has given the stoutest Man more Terror than an Army of Enemies, or a Pistol cock'd at his Breast: If there were no such Things as Spirits, then whence arises those dreadful Ideas? They cannot always be owing to the Prejudice of Education, nor would the bugbear Stories, told us in our Infancy by an old Nurse, have any Effect

in

in Maturity. No, no, that Spirits are sometimes permitted to render themselves visible to humane Sight is certain, as that we have immortal Souls, and whoever disbelieves the one, must most certainly be dubious of the other.

I AM far from wishing any Fellow-Creature should be put to Tryals they are unable to bear; yet I cannot forbear being pleased, when I hear a Person so arrogantly presuming, and depending on his Judgment, as in the Case above-recited, meets with something to humble his Self-sufficiency.

FOR my Part, I can impute the Arguments raised against Apparitions to nothing but an Affectation of Particularity, since there is no sound Reason to be given for this Opinion to be drawn from Religion, Morality or Nature; but on the contrary, they all concur to assure us there are no such Things, without the Testimony of occular Demonstration. I am sure Holy Writ, both in the *Old* and *New Testament*, gives us innumerable Proofs of it; few Histories are without some remarkable Examples of it, and the secret Indications we feel within ourselves, are perpetually confirming it.

I BELIEVE there are few real *Atheists* in the World, tho' too many, out of Ostentation of signalizing themselves, make so vile a Use of that Share of Understanding allowed them by

God

God, as to reason against him; and I dare say, the Number of those who disbelieve the Appearance of Spirits, so far as never to have the least Terror on that Account, would but little exceed the other more pernicious Tribe.

SOME there are who argue against this Truth, merely because they would not be thought to have any Tincture about them of what they imbibed in their Childhood; but, methinks, this is strangely ridiculous; are not the first Rudiments of all those Tenets we are most justly proud of, given us in our Childhood? We should, according to that Way of Reasoning, not begin to learn any thing till we are arrived at Maturity; and if the believing Spirits be a Notion which ought to be exploded, 'tis certainly an infinite Error to mention them at all in our Youth. The reading of *Glanville, Burton, Clarendon,* and, indeed, the Works of almost all the Great Men that ever wrote, must be entirely forbid, and a new Set of Books be found out to make the Furniture of our Libraries agreeable to the modern Way of Thinking.

I KNOW the main Objections against the Visibility of Spirits are these: *First,* The Impossibility there is in defining of what Nature they are. And *Secondly,* That supposing them to be Souls of the Deceased, *How,* says the Objector, *is it consonant to Religion, that the Blessed shall forsake Heaven, where all Tears are wiped from the*

Eyes, to concern themselves with the Affairs below? Or, if doomed to Misery, shall their Tortures be intermitted, and they have Liberty to return to the Place where they have committed their Crimes? But yet even this Argument, formidable as it may seem, methinks, 'tis easy to confute, without denying one Word concerning the unceasing Joys which the Virtuous enjoy, or the Pains of the Vicious, after their Departure from this Life.

As to the First, I grant it impossible for humane Understanding to comprehend of what Nature they are, but we are told, that there are infinite Degrees and Orders of Angels; may it not then be more than probable, as may be proved by *Lot*, and several of the Patriarchs, that the Business of some of them may be to visit this lower World, for Reasons only known to the Supream Director; And as for those dreadful Apparitions, which we cannot imagine to be any that is Good, does it not bear some Likelihood of Truth, that the fallen Angels, who, till the Day of final Judgment, are not locked up in their Adamantine Caverns, may be permitted to wander here, and sometimes render themselves visible for the Punishment or Admonition of those to whom they shall appear; but as the Certainty of this is what the most Learned cannot arrive at, what serves for an Objection, may as justly be made Use of in Defence.

Nor

Nor does the Suppofition, that they are really the Souls of the Deceafed, include any Thing of Profane or Irreligious in it. Even thofe Spirits, for any thing we know, may be allotted to the Bufinefs above-mentioned, fince all agree that Happinefs or Mifery is not compleated till the laft Day, 'tis enough if either to know it will be fo, which Knowledge all Souls, doubtlefs, are poffeffed of, immediately after leaving the Body, and, therefore, they may, with great Probability, be commiffioned to bring about Matters here, which require an extraordinary Meffenger.

I am not for fetting this down as a Thing to be depended on, 'tis what none can be affured of while in a State of Mortality: But I hope I may be allowed to fay there is nothing in fuch an Opinion abfurd, nor contrary to the Notions we ought to have of Things beyond our Comprehenfion.

That Spirits have the Power of making themfelves vifible, I am certain, and, that they are either commiffioned, or permitted to be fo by the moft High, none, who acknowledges a Deity will deny: It is not therefore our Bufinefs to enquire into their Nature, nor to difpute their Being, becaufe we cannot comprehend it. Man, while in Flefh, is, doubtlefs, the moft Inferior of rational Creation, and he ought to believe humbly

humbly what is revealed to him, and not presumptuously dive into, much less pretend to know, Secrets to which he can never arrive, till he has shot the Gulph of Death.

And, sure, nothing more testifies the Wisdom of the Divine Being, than continuing us in this Uncertainty! Were we to be informed, directly, what either the Joys of Heaven, or the Pains of Hell were, it would naturally destroy great Part of our Dependance on him: It is by *Faith* we are to be saved, and after *Conviction*, where is there need of *Faith?* Besides, should the Spirit of a vicious Person, who, after being guilty of innumerable Transgressions, at last find Mercy, thro' Repentance, inform us he were in a State of Happiness, might it not encourage the Sinner to go on in his Offences? Or, were a Person, seemingly Virtuous, tho', perhaps, guilty of some secret, great and unrepented Crime, appear to us in all the Horrors of Damnation, would it not stagger the Hope of the most Pious? It is, therefore, highly necessary those Things should be concealed from us, unless we could, also, see into the Reasons of the Almighty's Decree, to keep us from the two dangerous Extremes of Presumption and Despair.

But, to return to my Purpose: How many private Murders have been revealed by the Apparition of the murdered Person? I remember, *Beaumont* makes Mention of a Man, who being
appre-

apprehended on Suspicion, was about being cleared, when the Spirit, or Ghost, of the Deceased appeared, circled in Fire, before the Eyes of the Prisoner, and terrified him into an immediate Confession of the Fact, with all its Circumstances, of which, before, there was not the least Proof. I have, also, read in another Author, tho' his Name has now slipped my Memory, of a Woman, who being left a Widow, with one Son of about two Years old, soon after married a Kinsman of her late Husband's, and the next Heir to the Estate, (which was a very large one) in Case he had died without Issue; but not long surviving these second Nuptials, the Widower took it in his Head to become Master of the Estate; to which End, he sent the Child into a remote Country, and gave out, he was dead: Every thing was contrived in so artful a Manner, that no-body suspected the Deceit, and he enjoyed the Estate, by which he obtained a Lady of a considerable Fortune, with whom he was much enamoured, for his Wife: In a few Years he had several fine Children by her, and nothing seemed wanting to compleat his Happiness, yet did he grow so excessively melancholly, that every-body was surprized at his Behaviour; he even hated the Sight of his Wife, his Children, and every thing which it might be expected he should love. It is not to be doubted but that he was very much intreated to reveal the Cause of this so sudden Change in his Behaviour, yet nothing would prevail on him, till his Distemper

encreasing

encreasing in such Sort, as made every-body believe he could not long survive under it; at last, in a more than ordinary Confusion, he called for his Wife and Family about him, having, before, sent for two Clergymen of his Acquaintance, and in the Presence of them all, declared the Injury he had done his first Wife's Child, adding, *That for a Twelvemonth she had continued to appear to him, and that Day had threatened him in a most terrible Manner, if he persisted in his Injustice.* He then told them where he had disposed of the Child, who was then about twelve Years of Age, *with a poor Woman in* Wales, *whom he allowed no more than five Pounds a Year for the maintaining him*; confessing also, *That his Intent was to have put him out to some mean Trade, and never to have let him known his Name, or of what Family descended.* Every-body, but his Wife, applauded his Repentance; but she took the Imposition he had put on her, so ill, that she protested never to live with him more, and that Moment left his House: The young Heir, however, was immediately sent for to *London*, and Care taken of his Education, befiting his Birth and Fortune.

WHAT became of the Gentleman, I do not remember, nor is it to my Purpose, which is only to prove, that Heaven sometimes makes Use of supernatural Means to bring about extraordinary Events; and, as little as some People affect to believe this Truth, let them beware how they defraud the Innocent, or any way forfeit their Promife to the Dead, left they fhould be convinced, to their Coft, that the Things I have related are not impoffible.

But it would be the utmoft Prefumption in me, to expect any Arguments from my unlearned Pen, fhould prevail on Perfons deaf to thofe elaborate and elegant ones, which have wrote fo many large Volumes in the Defence of giving Credit to Apparitions: Nay, when the very Bible, which abounds in Examples of them, is not looked on as a fufficient Authority in this Point. Nothing can convince thofe who take a Pride in being obftinate, but occular Demonftration; to that, therefore, I leave them, and if fuch Conviction ever happens, let them thank themfelves, if they fuffer worfe by it than the more Timid, who are, at prefent, fo much the Subject of their Ridicule.

In Defiance of all may be faid in Oppofition, I do aver, that there are Apparitions; fome of the moft glorious, fome of the moft dreadful Kind, that all my Senfes have been Witnefs of their Force, and that, not only in Vifions in my Bed, but waking, and in the open Fields; and that many great and wonderful Things have, from my Childhood, been revealed to me by them: Nor do I conceal this from the World out of Fear of any thing they can fay againft me for it, but becaufe it is vain for me to hope my
Words

Words will have that Weight while I am living, as, I am certain, they will obtain when I am paſt the Cenſure, the Praiſe, or the Concern of any thing below.

HERE I will beg Leave to incert a merry Adventure which happened in my more juvinile Years, and may, perhaps, be diverting to my Readers after this grave and tedious Diſcourſe.

ABOUT Twenty five Years ago, there was a famous blind Man, of whom I had heard wonderful Stories, eſpecially concerning his being able to diſtinguiſh Colours, and playing at all Games on the Cards; and I expreſſing a great Deſire to ſee him, a Gentleman of my Acquaintance undertook to bring us together: Accordingly a Day was fixed, and he was to play three Games at All-Fours with me for a Guinea to be ſpent, and I was to have my own Cards. The appointed Day being arrived, both of us were punctual, neither of us failed, and each had his 'Squire to ſupply the Deficiency of our ſeveral Talents. A great deal of Company were there, and it occaſioned abundance of Laughter among them to ſee our Salutation. After a *Half-Pint of Brandy* round, I pulled out my Cards, and was very watchful, as I thought, yet, for all that, I was deceived: Before we went to Play, he would needs ſhew ſome Tricks; and it was a moſt ſurprizing Thing to me, to ſee him go directly to any Card I called for; he was very

arch

arch about Kings, Knaves, Politicks, and State-Affairs; but while he was amusing me this Way, his 'Squire marked all the Cards with a small Pin, so as not to be perceived by the Eye, but easily distinguished by the Touch, by a Person who depended wholly on feeling, as he, himself, shewed me afterwards.

At last, to Play we went, and he let me win the first Game, by way of Compliment, but he won the second and third; and as I began to find myself the forlorn Hope, I conveyed three of the Knaves into my Bosom, thinking, by them, to retrieve all; but I presently saw him laugh, and he told my Friend, *That I had three Knaves, and might take the fourth if I pleased, he would be at me for all that*; on which I threw up my Cards, owned the Wager lost, and contented myself with being the Game of the Company, as they called it.

My blind Man wondered how it could be possible to talk by Fingers, and said, *He would freely spend his Guinea to mine, to learn*: A Friend of mine soon took him up, and engaged to make us able to converse together that Way in half an Hour. Some of the Company believed this a Thing impossible, and several Wagers were laid upon it, but those who were of a contrary Opinion, were soon convinced, for the Gentleman made him immediately comprehend the Twenty-four Letters, which done, it was easy for

for him to put them into what Words he pleaſed; when he directed his Diſcourſe to me, and when I ſpoke to him, I had no more to do, than to touch his Fingers inſtead of my own: In fine, no two Perſons in Company could be more converſible with each other, than we were within the Time prefixed; on which, ſaid the blind Man, *I ſee by Feeling, and you hear by your Eyes.* He afterwards ſurprized every-body, by his being able to diſtinguiſh Colours only by rubbing the Cloath between his Fingers: A briſk Spark aſking him, *If he would not gladly change all for his Eyeſight?* he anſwered him, *That he would not*; and added, *That he believed, I, who ſaw ſo much, would readily change Talents with him:* On which, I told the Company, *That I would not loſe the Sight of the Sun, and a fine Woman, to be Emperor of the whole Globe; and, that I would be deprived of Legs and Arms, nay, endure Caſtration itſelf, rather than quit ſo valuable a Bleſſing as that of Sight.*

CHAP.

CHAP. XI.

On the GENII.

THAT every Man, from his Birth, is under the Direction of both a good and bad *Genius*, is as certain, as that by Air the Breath of Life is preserved; and according as either of these prevails, we are addicted to Virtue or to Vice, to Things which tend to our Happiness or Misery in this World also, as well as in the next; but of what Degree or Order these ministring Spirits are, is a Query to which the most learned can give no positive Solution.

THAT God has given his blessed Angels Charge over us, as we are more than once informed in Holy Writ; and that the fallen ones have Power to tempt, seduce, and prompt us to Mischief, the same undeniable Authority assures us; but whether they may properly be called the *Genii*, is a knotty Point, or whether there are not yet another Degree of instigating Spirits who preside over our Actions: if it be so, we

may

may be said to be influenced by three second Causes under Heaven to Happiness, *viz.* The Beneficient Planet which reigned at the Moment of our Nativity, the Guardian Angel, and the good *Genius*: As also by the Malevolent Aspect at our Birth, the Devil, and the ill *Genius*. If I may be allowed to give my Opinion, I think this Way of Reasoning rather confounds than clears the Dispute; for if we are under the Direction of a Guardian Angel, as few make any Difficulty of believing, I see no Necessity of a *Genius*, or rather they are both the same, and *Genius* is but another Name for Angel: As for any other intellectual Advisers, I look on them to be only our own Actions, which, according as they are, instigate and prompt us to Good or Evil.

The wisest of us all, however, can no more than guess; *While we remain in this Life, we see, as St. Paul says, through a Glass dimly, but when once we are arrived at Immortality, we shall distinguish clearly all those Things which at present seem so dark. How vain is it, therefore, to spend our Time in the Search of what is impossible to be found, or if it could, would probably avail us nothing!*

But to return to the Design of this Chapter. Though all Men are under the Guidance of these intellectual Intelligences, yet to very few have they made themselves visible, and when they have, it has been frequently in such Shapes as might rather create Aversion or Contempt, than Love

Love or Veneration. I knew a Person who never attempted to commit an ill Action, but something in the Form of a Bear appeared to him, and stared him in the Face; and whenever he went out of his House on any laudable Design, he was sure of seeing the same Shape go before him Step by Step, never turning, unless it was to warn him to go back, which, whenever it did, he knew there was something of Misfortune or Danger in the Way. This he had in many Things experienced; but one Time above the rest deserved his particular Regard, and is not unworthy a Place in this Treatise. As hs was on the Road travelling towards *Dunstable*, where he went every Year, having a small Estate in that Part, his Conductor, on a sudden, turned short upon him, and stood Cross-way; this very much amazed him, but being unwilling not to pursue his Journey, he quitted the Road and took the Field; but before he had proceeded many Paces, the Bear was before him, not peaceably marching on as his Guide or Harbinger, but as a Beast of Prey in act to tear him to Pieces and devour him; this so much frighted him, that he turned his Horse, and made what Haste he could back to a little House, where he had a little before called to drink at: There he alighted, which he had no sooner done, than he saw the Bear lie down quietly at the Door. He now perceived he had been but menaced into Safety, and filled with an imaginary Danger, to preserve him from a real one, though of what

Nature

Nature he could not guess, till having tarried where he was some Hours, a Gentleman was brought in, who had been robbed and mortally wounded by three Highwaymen, on that very Spot where the Bear had obliged him to turn back, and, according to the best Calculation of Time, not above two Minutes after he had left it.

Another Person, from whose own Mouth I also had the following Account, being one Night in Bed, was strangely disturbed by something which seemed to pull the Corner of the Sheet; he was a little surprized at first, but being naturally Courageous, he drew the Curtain, and by a Candle, which he had always burning in the Chimney, he saw a huge Rat, which ran several Times round the Bed, and in its Race still catched hold on the Sheet, and plucked it with uncommon Eagerness. The Gentleman taking it for a real material Rat, and having a kind of Aversion to those Vermin, jumped out of Bed, and drew his Sword, designing to kill it, but the Creature evaded the Blows, and though he thought several Times the Point was through the Body, yet did he still see it running about: After having disappointed him in this Manner, it made to the Door, and, as he thought, escaped under it; on which he turned the Spring, thinking to destroy this Interrupter of his Repose in the Stair-case, but he was presently inspired with other Thoughts, for on opening the Door,

such

such a terrible Smoak burst in upon him, as assured him the House was on Fire, and left him nothing to reflect on, but how to escape the Danger; he was going to run down Stairs, but had not gone half way, before he perceived the Flames had already seized all the lower Part, on which he had Presence enough of Mind to run back into his Chamber, which looking into the Garden, he threw himself out of the Window, and got over the Wall time enough to alarm the Neighbours, and by that Means preserved himself and many others, who else doubtless would have perished; none being lost but the careless Wretch who had occasioned this Conflagration, by setting a Scuttle-Basket of hot Cynders under a Dresser in the Kitchen, which presently taking Fire, consumed all that was near it; the Wench lying in a Settle-Bed just by, was, no doubt, immediately suffocated.

A STORY, no less surprising than either of these, I can aver the Truth of, being intimately acquainted with the Person principally concerned in it. This Gentleman having experienced the Frailties of the fair Sex, was an utter Enemy to Marriage; and, I am sure, I do not wrong him when I say, that till the Age of three or four and thirty, no Man was ever a greater Rake. He was, indeed, one of those whose Example made me wicked; we have fenced together, drank together, whored together, scowered the Watch together,

together, and, in fine, done every Thing together which distinguishes the Rattle from the Men of Consideration. But as these were only the Extravagancies of Youth, when he arrived at the Years I mentioned, he began to grow ashamed of his former Behaviour, and would often say, *That such a Conduct was not only an Offence to Heaven, but also to the Dignity of humane Reason*; in a Word, he threw off all his former Follies, discarded all his unreformed Companions, and became a perfect sober Man: Being such, and of a good Family, and a plentiful Estate, he had a great many Matches proposed to him; but though the Vices of his own Humour were entirely converted into Virtues, yet did his Aversion to Marriage still continue, not out of any Dislike of that State in itself, but having been guilty of wronging the Bed of many a deserving Man himself, he feared it would come home to him; and Cuckoldom being an Injury he knew himself unable to endure, without committing some desperate Act, he thought it best not to put it to a Venture. This made him refuse all the Offers that were made to him, and it was the Opinion of everybody, as well as of himself, that courting any Woman for a Wife, would be the last Thing he would do. But at length he began to find, that though he had thrown off all his loose Behaviour, he could not do the same by his amorous Inclinations, and the Fires of Youth not being extinguished in him, he continually wished

there

there were a Possibility of his being assured of a Woman's Virtue, but there was none, for the Timidity of his Humour, in this Point, made him look on the most innocent Freedoms of that Sex as Criminal; and though he was acquainted with many Ladies of undoubted Chastity, he could not find in his Heart to place so great a Dependance on any one of them, as to trust his Honour and Peace of Mind in her Keeping, till one Summer, being at the Country House of a Relation of his, he saw a Farmer's Daughter who lived in the Neighbourhood; the Girl was very beautiful, and not exceeding sixteen Years of Age, and seemed possessed of such an innate Modesty, that she could not restrain her Blushes if even spoke to by a Man; but a Kiss, or the least Touch of her Hand threw her into a Trembling. This Behaviour was sufficient to charm my Friend; he was now certain he had found a Virgin, and he thought he might depend on his own Watchfulness over her to preserve her uncorrupted after she became his Wife. As he was entirely the Master of himself and Fortune, he asked no Advice if he should marry her; and it is not to be doubted but such a Proposal was acceptable to her Parents, seeing the great Affection he had for her; they, however, took so much Advantage of it as to demand a Settlement for her, in Case he should die without Children, to which he readily complied, and the Day being fixed for drawing the Writings, he brought a Lawyer to the Farmer's mer's House; when every Thing was ready for him to sign, the Window being open, a Raven flew in, and with her Beak snatched the Pen out of his Hand, as he was that Moment putting it to the Parchment. So odd an Accident surprized the whole Company, but most the intended Bridegroom; however, loath to shew himself superstitious, he took another Pen, on which the Raven returned, and, fluttering over the Table, croaked several Times, and with her Wings and Claws threw down the Writings, and made, as it were, a kind of an Effort to tear them. It is impossible to express the Consternation every-body now felt, but the Gentleman was so much shocked, that he became exceeding sick, insomuch, that he was unable, if yet he had an Inclination, to set his Hand at this Time. It was also the Opinion of every one, that it should be deferred, though, perhaps, none could tell the Meaning of so particular an Omen, yet all agreed it was not a good one.

My Friend was so much disordered, that they persuaded him to tarry all Night, telling him, they hoped the next Day would recover him, and also bring Promises of a better Fate: He was easily persuaded, and they put him to Bed, but his discontented Thoughts quitted him not there; he could not reflect on what had happened, without believing there was something miraculous in it; and tho' he was infinitely in
Love

Love with the Girl, not all his good Opinion was sufficient to make him flatter himself with the Hope of Happiness with her. Finding it impossible to sleep, and it being a fine Moonlight Night, he put on his Cloaths, and resolved to pass the Remainder of it in the Garden; but, as he was passing thro' the Yard which led thither, he heard Voices in a Barn, close to which he was obliged to go; Curiosity made him stand to listen what had brought any-body there, at an Hour in which he imagined none awake but himself, and easily perceived, that one of those who spoke, was his Mistress, and the Person who accompanied her, a Rival more beloved than himself; he heard the Words, *My Dear,—my Love, and my Life,* several Times repeated, before he offered to interrupt the Conversation, but his Patience being, at length, put to the Rack, and reflecting, that whatever he should say of this the next Day, would be denied, and his Accusation taken as Malice, or Inconstancy, he burst suddenly into the Barn, and found this seeming innocent Maid with her Partner, who was no other than one of her Father's Plowmen, in a Posture the most provoking to a Lover; in fine, in one not fitting to describe, but convincing to him that saw it, how grosly he had been cheated, if he had married her. They both fell on their Knees, and begged he would be secret; but he was then too much exasperated to promise any thing, and flinging from them, returned to his Bed, acknowledging, the

Raven

Raven had been his Guardian-Angel. When he came, after, to reflect coolly on it, his Rage was succeeded by Contempt; but, as he had loved her, forbore exposing her, and only telling her Father, *That, for some private Reasons, he could not marry*, took his everlasting Leave of the whole Family.

I HAVE known several of these, who, like Sir *Solomon Single*, in the Comedy, are sure of having a Virgin for their Wife, provided they make Choice of one that is very young, and very silly, and have found themselves deceived on the Proof, tho' I know of none, but this Gentleman, whose Good Angel so immediately interposed, or, to speak more justly, none who were so ready to obey its Admonitions.

I COULD present my Reader with innumerable Instances of Persons who have seen and conversed with their good *Genii*, but have neither heard, nor read of many, to whom an ill one has been so familiar; and concerning the Reason of this, I once met with a very learned Dispute between two, who were both great Philosophers, and Divines of the Church of *England*: The one maintained, that it was owing to the great Goodness of Providence to us Mortals, that the ill *Genii* had not the Power of being visible, because they would, doubtless, appear in such a Form, as must drive the Person who beheld them, to Distraction. The other, tho' far from

taking

taking from the Mercy of the Supreme Being, would not allow it laid any such Restriction, but that the Evil Spirits themselves chose rather to infuse their pernicious Doctrines into the Ears of the Mind, than any way render themselves perceptible by the Organs of the Body: To prove this, he added, That according to the Notion of the most learned Men on these supernatural Beings, it is permitted them to assume what Shape they please, and they might, therefore, appear in the most persuasive and agreeable, as easily as in the most dreadful one.

I will not pretend to enter into Secrets of this Kind, nor to determine which of these Gentlemen was really in the Right, tho', according to all humane Probability, the latter had the best of the Argument: But shall conclude this Chapter with two Assertions, which are all I dare be positive in; first, That every Man, from his Birth, is divided between the Influences of a good and bad *Genius*, under whatsoever Names or Orders they may be distinguished; and that, tho' few have conversed with them any otherwise than intellectually, and, in a manner, altogether imperceptible to the Senses, yet, in the Moment of departing this Life, they are visible, and either mitigate the Agonies of Death, or add new Horrors to it, according to the Power either of them has had over the Actions of the dying Person. Of this I could give many Examples from the Sacred Text, and the Judgment

ment of the moſt learned, as well Chriſtian as prophane Authors; but whoever carefully obſerves the Emotions of a Perſon's Face juſt in that Criſis, will diſcern enough not to ſtand in Need of any other Teſtimonial.

CHAP. XII.

On the SECOND SIGHT.

IT will, doubtleſs, be expected that I, who have the Gift of *Second Sight*, ſhould ſay ſomething by way of defining it; but, tho' to do that is utterly impoſſible, yet, to gratify the Curioſity of my Readers, I ſhall make no Secret of any thing concerning it, that is in my Power to reveal.

Firſt, THEN, it cannot be denied, that the *Second Sight* is a palpable and immediate Inſpiration from the ſupreme Source of all Knowledge: The Perſon poſſeſſed of it, has no Warning of its coming on, or quitting him; he ſees, and comprehends Millions of Things at once, which other Mortals are incapable even of conceiving; and which he himſelf, who diſcerning them clearly

clearly with his bodily Eyes, has not the Power of defcribing.

Secondly, It is not to be learned, nor acquired, by the moſt ſtrenuous Application; it laughs at all the Efforts of Wiſdom, and puts to Shame all humane Knowledge; it is equally powerful in Childhood as in Maturity, nor abates of its Force in enervating Old Age; the Infirmities of the Body have no Effect on it, but, on the contrary, it renders ſtrong, for the Time, thoſe Organs of the Senſes thro' which it operates.

Thirdly, It brings the moſt diſtant Objects to Hand, Mountains, Rivers, Seas, are no Impediment to its Diſcernment, nor can what is acted in the moſt dark Receſs, eſcape its Penetration: It even looks beyond this World, and deſcries thoſe Beings who owe their Origin to ſomething above Nature; the perpetual Combats between the good and bad *Genii*; the Revolution of Orbs too diſtant for the Teleſcope's Diſcovery; the Fates of whole Kingdoms, as well as of particular Perſons, are its ordinary Entertainments; in fine, there is nothing ſhut from the *Second Sight*, but the Divine Myſteries of that Heaven of Heavens, where ſits enthroned the awful and unutterable Majeſty of Him who made theſe Wonders.

To be poſſeſſed, at all Times, of this Inſpiration, this ſurprizing, this unſpeakable Emanation
of

of the Divine Prescience, what would it be but to arrive at Immortality before our Time? But, alas! it comes upon us but by Starts, it is with us, it is gone, and, like a sudden Thought, is lost in Clouds, nor can our utmost Art recal it, till all at once, and e'er we are aware, it returns, and with the same Velocity vanishes again.

MANY of my Consulters have told me, they extremely envied me this Gift; that they would give all they were worth in the World, to be possessed of it in the same Degree I am; and that they thought it a Blessing infinitely superior to any thing Humanity could receive; but, tho' I should think it profane in me to repine at the Will of Heaven, and have profited as much by this Gift, as, perhaps, any that ever had it, yet, I cannot but confess, it has frequently presented me with Objects so very astonishing and terrible, as have made me wish, within myself, it would depart from me for ever.

SOMETIMES, when surrounded by my Friends, such as *Anthony Hammond*, Esq; Mr. *Philip Horneck*, Mr. *Phillips*, Mr. ———, Mrs. *Centlivre*, Mrs. *Fowk*, Mrs. *Eliza Haywood*, and other celebrated Wits, of which my House, for some Years, has been the general Rendezvous, a good Bowl of Punch before me, and the Glass going round in a constant Circle of Mirth and good Humour, I have, in a Moment, beheld Sights

K 2 which

which has froze my very Blood, and put me into Agonies that difordered the whole Company.

Even in my Bed, where, after the Fatigues of the Day were over, I hoped Repofe, my Chamber has been filled with Company, the moft fhocking to humane Nature. In the Fields my Solitude has been, in the fame Manner, difturbed; in the Park, when moft crouded with the gay World, I have feen among the *Belles* and *Beaux*, fuch Objects, as, could they have difcerned as well as I, it would have converted their Pride into Confufion, and their Sprightlinefs into Anguifh.

Nor that the *Second Sight* affords only Occafions of Dread; all that the moft raptured Imagination can form of Delight, falls fhort of thofe Heavenly Vifions which have, fometimes, danced before my Eyes; and, were it not for the exquifite Happinefs of the latter, the former would be impoffible to be fuftained with Life.

This is all the Defcription I am able to give of *Second Sight*; nor do I believe it in the Power of any-body to do it more fully. As I have been poffeffed of it from my Childhood, the various Objects it prefents, are much more familiar to me, and confequently lefs aftonifhing, than to a Perfon who but lately received the Infpiration: I, therefore, may be allowed to fay, that what I am unable to reveal concerning it, none elfe

can

can pretend to do, without being guilty of an Impofition on thofe they fhall endeavour to gain Credit from.

CHAP. XIII.

On the VIRTUES *of the* LOADSTONE, *and fome other choice Curiofities in Nature.*

HAVING in a former Chapter made Mention of the moſt terrible Fits, which, for feveral Years together, perplexed me, and fometimes for whole Days took from me the Power of doing any thing for the Service of thoſe who came to confult me at that Time, and being now greatly relieved from them, I think it my Duty to let the World know by what Means I received fo peculiar a Mercy. After having effayed all that Phyſick could do, and finding not the leaſt Benefit, I gave myſelf over as incurable; till one Night my good *Genius*, in the Shape in which he ordinarily appeared to me, came to my Bed-Side, and informed me, that by wearing a *Loadſtone* I fhould have Eaſe. I then fet myſelf feriouſly to confider its Virtues, and wondered how I could have been fo long Stupid, as not to make the Tryal of what, in numberleſs Cafes, I had
expe-

experienced the good Effects of on others, though in Relation to different Diseases and Casualties.

The *Loadstone*, of all Things under Heaven, has this peculiar Quality, to attract and draw off at the same Time. The Person who wears it, is not only defended from the Infection of any Ill from Abroad, but is also certain of the Love and Esteem of his Fellow-Creatures. Of all Magnetics in Nature, without the Assistance of Art, it is certainly the most effectual, and there is scarce any Contingency of Life, wherein it is not of excellent Use.

In Maladies it chiefly is of Force on those which relate to the Head and Eyes, such as Epileptic or convulsive Fits, and Dimness of Sight, occasioned either by too dry or too moist a Brain.

It is admirably serviceable to those who labour under the Malignity of an Evil Tongue, and even (by God's Blessing) repels the Efforts of Witchcraft in great Measure.

As to its Virtues, they are numberless, and I might fill a Volume, and not recount half of them; it shall therefore suffice to say, *That whoever wears it, if destined to good Fortune, he shall find his Happiness encrease by the Possession of it; and if ill, an Abatement of his Woes.* This has

has been experienced by Hundreds, and I doubt not, but when this comes to be in Print, a great many of them will readily avouch it.

I AM sensible, however, that several Persons have carried a *Loadstone* about them, without finding the least good Effect proceed from it; but this does not at all lessen the Virtues of this admirable Magnetic, as I will make appear very plainly.

First, AMONG the many Impositions practised in this great City, there is none more gross than that on the Account of the *Loadstone*. I knew a Man who got an Estate by selling a compound Matter of his own Composing for it; how then could any Virtue proceed from it? nothing being more difficult in reality to come by than a *pure Loadstone*.

Secondly, THERE is a great deal owing to the Setting and Arming the *Loadstone*, when a true one, so as to render it capable of operating in its full Force and Vigour; and to do this, with Skill, requires Instruction from something more than a Mechanick. There is but one Man in *England* who is possessed of this Art, and was taught it by myself, under an Obligation to work in that Manner for no other Person but me, or those to whom I should bequeath my Secrets after my Decease.

The *Ægyptian Loadstones* are infinitely the best, for which Reason, I purchased a good Number of them, of a Merchant to whom I communicated their Virtues, and engaged him to procure them for me; but as they cost more than twice the Price of those which are ordinarily made Use of by Mariners, it has given a Handle to my Enemies, to make those, who judge but by Appearances, believe I imposed on my Customers, by taking from them, what they call an extravagant Rate: But I have this Consolation, as in many other Things, that the Persons themselves who pay'd the Money are of another Opinion, and value the Favour I did them, as it indeed deserves.

As I have always made it my Study to oblige my Clients, I have had it in my Power to do them many more Services than could be expected from the *Second Sight* alone, by conversing with all the *Virtuosi* I heared of in any Part of the World, and obtaining from them many choice and valuable Secrets. I have corresponded to *Ægypt*, *China*, *Turky*, and even from the *Indies* have learned Things, which many who, I doubt not, will read this Book, have experienced the Benefit of; but I would not be thought too partial to my own Country, when I avow, that my most curious Discoveries were made me by a Gentleman born in *Scotland*, and never out of it in his Life. But to give my
Reader

Reader a clearer Insight into the Obligations I have to him, I shall transcribe a Letter I received from him in his own Words, being an Answer to one I had sent him.

SIR,

*E*XCUSES *for the Non performance of a Promise, have more the Air of Complaisance than Friendship. Therefore, as it was not in my Power to procure the Rarities you desired, in so short a Time as I imagined, I chose rather to deprive myself of the Pleasure, which a Correspondence with you affords, than raise your Expectations with the Sight of a Letter from me, which, when open'd, would have given you so severe a Disappointment: But the hearty Zeal I have to serve you, and through you to do Good to my Fellow-Creatures, having at last surmounted all Difficulties, I shall now, with an inexpressible Satisfaction, return to that Happiness, the Reasons above-mentioned, have for so long an Interval debarred me from pursuing.* ⸺

I HAVE sent you a pretty large Quantity of the finest Coraline *the Isle of* Sky *affords. You know the other Virtues of it so well, that I need not trouble you with a Repetition of them; but the most eminent* Physician *and* Virtuoso *of these Parts, has lately discovered a new and wonderful Effect which it is capable of performing, to which, I believe, you are yet a Stranger: In the Box which contains it, you will find the* Recipe, *and proper Directions for the*

Manage-

Management of it, for a certain Malady therein mentioned. ———

WITH incessant Labour and Application, I have also procured some of the miraculous Black Bean; an Amulet, which those who profess themselves the greatest Enemies to what we call Superstition, are fond of keeping by them, and far from being ashamed of doing so. Your fair Clients will, doubtless, rejoice (when they shall know the prodigious Effects that a little of the Powder of one of these Beans will produce) to have it in their Power to compass their Desires so easily. ———

WITH the rest of the Gargoe, there is also twelve Phials of the Cleft-Rock Water, by Kinghorn, which, I am certain, will be of infinite Service to you in your wonderful Experiments. ———

THE Ship is ready to set Sail, and one of the Men impatiently attends to be dispatched, which prevents my enlarging at this Time, and I must beg leave to conclude, with assuring dear Mr. Campbel, that

I am,

His very sincere Friend,

and humble Servant,

A. L.

P. S.

P. S. *I have sent you a Box of* Eagle Stones *by Mr.* Gordon Whitchet, *so famous to prevent Miscarriages. I thought them too valuable to trust to the Mercy of the Seas, as, indeed, all the other Things are, but had no Opportunity to send any more by Land. Once more Adieu. Write to me on the Receipt of this.*

It never was my Nature to deny the Favours I receive, nor do I think it any Diminition of my own Merit, to acknowledge, that many of the wonderful Things I have done, have been owing to the curious Inquisitions of my learned Friends; nor will I pretend to appropriate any more to myself, than the Power of foretelling Events, and giving Advice in what Manner it is best to behave in them.

As for the admirable Virtues of the *Black Bean*, they would seem incredible, even to myself, had I not so frequently beheld the Proof. A certain Lady, whose Name I shall forbear to mention, has Reason to bless my Acquaintance with the Gentleman above; for (after being forsaken, slighted, nay, almost despised, for the Space of several Years, by a Person who had beguiled her of her Innocence and Reputation) she had not worn this *Amulet* full one and twenty Days, before her Lover returned full of Penitence for his past Offences, and more enamoured than

than ever : In fine, he put an End to her Shame and Sorrow, by publickly making her his Wife.

The *Coraline*, duly prepared, is no lefs wonderful; it renders fertile the fteril Womb, and brings back the Vigour of Youth in almoft old Age.

I should not omit the miraculous Things have been brought about by the *Cleft-Rock* Water, but that it being now impoffible to be attained, I will not give my Readers that Regret; the Knowledge of its Virtues would of confequence raife in their Minds, for the Lofs of fo excellent a Spring, which, for thefe two Years, has been dried, or, at leaft, ftopped up in fuch a Manner, as leaves no Hope of ever being able to explore it any more.

The good Effects of the *Eagle Stone* on pregnant Women are too commonly known to lay me under any Neceffity of repeating them: But as the right ones are very hard to be got, I would have all, who ftand in Need of them, be careful in the Purchafe, becaufe it is not only lofing the Benefit which might acrue from the Ufe of them, but the Stone which, I am very certain, has been impofed on fome People for an *Eagle Stone*, tho' it exactly refembles it in Form and Colour, being carried about a Woman, produces an Effect quite contrary to what is expected from it; and is as certain in its Operation a pernicious

Way,

Way, as the other is in a beneficial one. This I think is my Duty to inform the Publick, it being a rare Secret, and known but to very few.

IF it shall please the Almighty to continue me a few Years longer in this World, I shall make it my Care to procure a sufficient Store of these valuable Commodities, not only to furnish my good Consulters with during my natural Life, but also to leave some behind me with my Wife, in Case they should be inquired after, as I doubt not but they will, by many after my Decease; especially the *Loadstones*, because it has been evidently proved. The effectual Sort are to be had no where but of me; nor will I fail, by God's Leave, to prepare a considerable Quantity of my Sympathetic Powder, which, tho' I do not pretend to cure Wounds at Distance with, yet has been often found of Service for the Cure, or, at least, the Ease of Pains in the Mind: *It being*, to use the Words of a certain Lady who experienced it, *the best Balsam Nature ever produced to heal a bleeding Heart*; Nor, indeed, could I dye entirely at Peace with myself, if I should neglect so sovereign a Remedy as I know this to be.

CHAP.

CHAP. XIV.

Containing some EXAMPLES *of the* UNREASONABLE THINGS *frequently required of me.*

TO such a Height does the Curiosity, the Ambition, or the Malice of some People transport them, that, as they often say, *They would, indeed, go to the Devil to obtain their Ends*; and so silly are they, withal, as to imagine they need but ask and have, tho', in my Opinion, the Devil is least busy about those who so much desire to be acquainted with him: But Raillery apart; I had once a Consulter on an Occasion so very extraordinary, that, I think, it well deserves a Place in these Remarks, to the End, that unprejudiced Persons may see how little I have been inclinable to deceive those who put Confidence in me, and how strangely I have, sometimes, been put to it, to bring People to a right Notion of themselves, or what they ought to do I shall, therefore, as I have all the Papers that passed between us, by me, set down the Conversation, in the very Words it happened.

AFTER

AFTER, then, the accustomed Fee was paid me, and I had wrote her Name, (for that is a Proof of my Art, which is expected from me by all Degrees of People) she began in this Manner.

Woman. I AM now convinced you know as much as I was informed you did, and, therefore, I shall not trouble you with asking any other Questions, for you must understand, my Affair with you is of another Nature; but you must be secret.

D. C. IT is not my Way to betray the Secrets intrusted to me: I am the same as a Confessor in that.

Woman. I HAVE heard so, and that makes me confide in you; but you must, also, promise to do what I desire.

D. C. You may depend on that, if in the Compass of my Art.

Woman. YES, yes, I know it is in your Power, or I would not have come to you.

D. C. IF you think so, make no more Delays, I am ready to serve you.

Woman. You must know, a Relation of mine died about three Years ago, and left me a handsome Legacy, but the Rogues of Executors put off the Payment from Time to Time, with frivolous Excuses, knowing I cannot hold out a Law-Suit with them; I having been sick, and out of Business for a great while, and driven to
great

great Straits: In short, I am not able to scrabble any longer, and am resolved to sell myself to the Devil for a certain Time, if he will give me Money to recover my Legacy, and to do some other Things.

D. C. EXPLAIN what you mean by that Word selling yourself for a Time, and I will give you my Answer.

Woman. I WONDER you should be so dull of Apprehension; why, it must be to the lower Regions, I do not desire to stay a great while here, and am afraid of nothing: I am fully resolved to do it, if such a Thing can be done, which I am persuaded it may, and that you can put me in a Way how to do it: I earnestly beg, therefore, that you will, and that with all Speed, for every Moment is a Loss to me.

D. C. You strangely amaze me, but I hope you are not in earnest.

Woman. I DO not know why you should think so, I assure you I am; but I suppose you are so scrupulous because I have not offered you a competent Fee; but, believe me, I have tried all the Means I could to raise five Pounds for you, tho' I could no Ways do it; but you may depend on me, that as soon as the Bargain is made, and I have received the Money, you shall have fifty Pounds; therefore, pray dispatch it, that I may be at Ease.

D. C. AND have you considered how terrible a Thing it is to sell your Soul to everlasting Perdition, for a little transitory Pleasure?

Woman.

Woman. Nothing in it, I value not myself; I must and will do it.—I have no other Way,--when I have done that, I shall have Money to pay you and other People, and to live handsomely; —so pray make no more Scruples, I shall always esteem you, and be grateful, only be as speedy as you can, for it will be worse by this Day Week, if it be not done.

D. C. What do you mean by worse?

Woman. To be plain, I am not able to endure the Misery I am in any longer, and if I do not remedy it, as I can no otherwise than by this Means, I am resolved to hang myself.

D. C. Truly, as you say, that would be giving yourself to the Devil for nothing.

Woman. Therefore, if ever you did, or ever will do any thing as long as you live, I beg you will do this for me, and you shall have fifty Pounds.

D. C. I thought, since the Days of *Francis Spira*, and Doctor *Faustus*, no such Wickedness had ever entered into the Heart of Man, much less of Woman, whose Sex, for the most Part, renders her more soft and timid; Go Home and pray; for the Devil has already taken too great Possession of you, without giving Money for it, and it must be only the most sincere Penitence can unlose his Hold.

Woman. I wonder you should talk so; I never was inclined to any Sort of Wickedness in my Life; it is mere Necessity drives me to do this, and if Heaven had thought fit to give me what I want, I should never have thought of having Recourse to Hell.

D. C. Thus Mortals profanely tax the Bounty of their Creator, as if infinite Wisdom could be fathomed by humane Penetration: The Misfortunes you are under, are of your own seeking, they proceed from want of Faith, and Resignation; endeavour to reform your Heart, read the Holy Bible, and pray against the Temptations of the Devil, and, I will answer, you will either have better Fortune, or bear what you have with more Content.

Woman. If I thought there was a Possibility of living easy in the World, I would try what I could do.

D. C. Dependance on the Will of Heaven will make every thing easy to you; but, I would have you have Recourse to some able Divine, I am certain it would give you great Relief: As for what you desire of me, I would not have a Hand in it for all the Riches in the World.

Woman. Well, Sir, I will take your Advice; but if I should find no Benefit by the Means you propose, I shall certainly make myself away.

D. C. There is no Danger of it, if you are sincere in your Conversion, and willing to improve the Benefit you will receive from such a Behaviour.

Woman. I will try; for, I confess, I am a little shock'd that you, who must certainly deal with the Devil, by the Things you foretel, should
think

think it so sad a Thing to have any Business with him.

D. C. As for that Mistake, it may be rectified another Time; but, if you observe my Directions, you will be ready to confess, they proceeded not from the Devil, or any of his Agents: Therefore delay not, but be as zealous and impatient in this good Work, as you were, lately, in the Pursuit of the most horrid and detestable one.

Woman. I shall, and, whatever Progress I make, you shall know: I will wait on you again in a few Days.

Here she took her Leave, and according to her Promise, came to me again in about a Fortnight, intirely altered in her Way of thinking, and told me, *She owed not only her Satisfaction of Mind in this Life, but the Hope of her eternal Salvation also, in the next, in a great Measure to what I had said to her.*

Another Day I was accosted by one of the most lovely young Women I had ever seen in my Life, but looked extremely pensive and melancholly. I easily read, at first View, the Misfortune which had occasioned it, but had not the least Guess of the Request she had to make me for the Relief of it, which I shall set down, also, in in the Terms she expressed it: After I had let her know I was sensible she had resigned her Honour to the deluding Artifices of a certain great Man

Man, whose Name, with her own, I also, according to Custom, was obliged to write at full-Length.

Young Lady. I had not suffered my Virtue to become a Prey to his enchanting Tongue many Days, before I heard, by Accident, that he kept a Mistress, by whom he had several Children, and was so extremely fond of, that there was not any Possibility of his quitting her: This News made me almost distracted; the first Time I saw him, after it, I burst into Tears, and upbraided him with the Deceit he had been guilty of to me: He seemed a little shocked, but, in the End, confessed, there was a Lady whom he had had a long Intimacy with, but swore a thousand Oaths, that his Passion for her was now degenerated into a cold Esteem, or, at best, a mere Friendship; and that all his warmer Inclinations were intirely devoted to my Charms. Yet, notwithstanding this, he is scarce one Day without seeing her, and I have not a Visit from him above once a Week, and sometimes not so often; and I was told by one that knows him very well, and, I am sure, would not be guilty of uttering an Untruth, that he declares to all his Friends, *That if ever he marries, she shall be the Woman*. Now, Sir, I would fain have your Opinion, whether there be any Possibility of getting the Better of this Rival, and I will then tell you what I would have done.

D. C. SHE

D. C. She seems to have got faft hold of his Heart; the Children he has by her, endear her to him, and fhe is a Woman of Prudence and Difcretion.

Y. Lady. Why then does he not keep conftant to her? Why did he take fo much Pains to betray me?

D. C. He is a Man of Wit and Pleafure, and they are for all the fine Ladies, tho' they may be more particularly attached to one.

Y. Lady. Then all the Men of Wit and Pleafure are no better than Villains, —— but I have thought of a Way to triumph over her, if you will be fo good to afford me your Affiftance.

D. C. As how, fair Lady?

Y. Lady. I would have you fet fome Spell upon her, that fhould make her grow ugly: I have been told, that there are Things to be done, which will make a Perfon lofe their Complexion, Hair, and Teeth; I would have her as deformed as poffible, and if once her Beauty was gone, his Honour would never prevail above his Inclination.

D. C. I will not flatter you; though fhe is handfome, 'tis not the Charms of her Perfon, fo much as of her Mind, that have bound her to him; in fine, fhe has preferved him by her good Conduct, as you have loft him by the contrary; and though I fhould agree to do as you would have me, I am certain you would not be a Jot the better beloved for it.

Y. Lady. I do not know what you mean; pray what have I done to leſſen his Affections? I am ſure I love him to Diſtraction.

D. C. You do ſo; but that is not the Caſe: More Women loſe their Lovers by loving them too much than too little; not that Love deſtroys Love, unleſs beſtowed on a vile Object indeed. But where there is a great deal of Paſſion, and little Conduct, it makes a Woman guilty of Indecorums, which muſt infallibly leſſen the Eſteem of a Man of Senſe; and I would not give one Farthing for that Sort of Affection which is without Eſteem.

Y. Lady. You argue very juſtly; but he pretended ſuch an Infinity of Tenderneſs to me, that all I could do was no more than a Return.

D. C. I speak not of your Behaviour to him when you were alone together; I do not think a Woman can be too fond when there are no Eyes but thoſe of her Lover to be Witneſs of it. But I mean, you have been too open to other People. Your Paſſion for him, made you talk perpetually on him; you have watched at the Door and Window for his paſſing by in his Coach, and have called your Companions to look at him; in fine, you have taken a Pride in revealing what it would have been greater Diſcretion not to have given any Reaſon to ſuſpect: And when a Woman loſes all Regard for her own Honour, a Man is apt to eſteem her Affection as little.

Y. Lady.

Y. Lady. IF that be the Fault, she, whom he is much enamoured with, is guilty of the same; for, I am sure, all the Town is sensible of his Intrigue with her.

D. C. THE Circumstance is quite different: They were intimate for a long Time before it was known, and it was from himself that it was first discovered: besides, where there are Children, it is morally impossible to maintain a perpetual Secresy. I only say, it lessens a Woman's Character in the Opinion of her Lover, when she begins to seem careless what the World says of her.

Y. Lady. WELL, if I could but draw off his Affection from her, I would not care for any thing: I beg, therefore, that you will contrive some Way to do it, and I will make you all the Satisfaction you can desire.

D. C. THE only Way to do it, is, by increasing his Affection to yourself, and the Means I have already prescribed, if you think fit to follow them.

Y. Lady. IT is now too late to pretend there is nothing between us; all my Acquaintance know it; even my Father is no Stranger to it; poor Man, it has half broke his Heart.

D. C. I KNOW it, and, methinks, you should be sorry you have been so publick in it.

Y. Lady. MY Sorrow now would avail nothing. But tell me; is there no Way to plague this happy Rival?

D. C. I will not deceive you; it is out of your Power.

Y. Lady. No, I can do it, and without your Affiſtance: I will tell all that has happened to a Perſon, who I know will carry the News immediately to her. That will certainly make her mad; ſhe muſt tremble at the Thoughts of his having a new Miſtreſs, and, I dare believe, by what I have heard, ſomething more agreeable.

D. C. I have already told you, it is not her Perſon ſhe depends upon, but upon thoſe Embelliſhments of the Mind, which only can maintain a laſting Paſſion: You will but expoſe yourſelf, and become leſs valuable in his Eyes.

Y. Lady. I do not care, ſo I but give her Pain.

D. C. It will be a very tranſient one. You are not the firſt he has ſometimes diverted himſelf with, yet has his Heart, after ſtraying, returned to its Home in her Boſom with redoubled Fondneſs: This ſhe is ſo ſenſible of, that it would be altogether in vain to think to give her any Affliction that way: In ſhort, he is a Man more juſtly deſerving the Character of Great from his admirable Underſtanding, than Birth, Eſtate, or Employments, though all of them are above the common Level of Mankind; and there is no Way to make your Rival unhappy, but behaving in ſuch a Manner, as ſhall make him judge you merit his Affection beſt.

Y. Lady. Well, I will endeavour to follow your Advice.

This

This was the Sum of what paſſed at our firſt Converſation; but my Counſel had not the ſame good Effect on her, as in the preceeding Example. She had but little beſides Beauty to recommend her, and that ſoon loſt its Reliſh with a Man of her Lover's fine Senſe. I was frequently plagued with her Importunities, but had it not in my Power to ſerve her, ſhe having neither the Capacity, nor Diſpoſition, to do any thing which might have contributed to my Endeavours, and ſhe ſoon fell into that moſt wretched Circumſtance of an abandoned Miſtreſs, while the other Lady glories in having eſtabliſhed a laſting and unalterable Affection in the Heart of one of the fineſt Gentlemen of the preſent Age: So prevalent is Truth, Tenderneſs, good Humour, and good Senſe, over thoſe happy enough to diſtinguiſh and value ſuch Virtues according to their Due.

But I had one Adventure, which I never remember without Aſtoniſhment at the mingled Wickedneſs and Folly of ſome People; it was with the Wife of a *Holland* Trader: This Woman loved her Huſband with ſo troubleſome a Paſſion, that whenever he was out of her Sight, ſhe imagined he was with another Woman, and would be guilty of ſo many Extravagancies, as would ſeem incredible to any who were not Witneſſes of them.

This

This Woman came to me, in one of her Agitations, and having been satisfied in my Skill, as to telling her Name, and the Name of her Husband, with the Time of her Marriage, she wrote to me in the following Manner.

Woman. Sir, I desire you will shew me, in a Glass, what my Husband is doing now, for I have Reason to believe he is with some Slut or other.

D. C. What Advantage would that be to you, if you knew it?

Woman. You must tell me also, where he is, that I may go and tear her Eyes out.

D. C. And would not that provoke him to use you ill?

Woman. He dares not say a Word; for he knows I would go to the Devil for my Revenge: But it is in your Power to do me a greater Service than all this.

D. C. What is it? I will serve you in any thing that is lawful.

Woman. This is nothing but what is lawful and just; I would have you fright my Husband from going to any of these wicked Creatures any more.

D. C. If you send him to me, I will let him see the Folly of it, if he be really guilty.

Woman. He will not regard any thing that is said to him on that Score, nor will own any of his Tricks; but I would have you raise a Spirit
to

to haunt him whenever he goes out of the House, and then he would be glad to keep at Home.

D. C. But have you any Proof that he is false to your Bed.

Woman. No, I want you to give me that.

D. C. But why do you suspect him?

Woman. Because he often stays abroad a full half-Hour longer than Business detains him, and pretends he met some Friend by the Way: Sometimes he comes Home very much out of Humour, and does not so much as kiss me; and when I complain of his Unkindness, he makes an Excuse, forsooth, that his Affairs go wrong. In short, I have taken Notice, that he sighs very much of late, and, I am sure, it is for some Whore or another: Therefore, I beg you will raise a Spirit that shall appear to him in a very frightful Shape, and make him glad to come, as fast as he can, to his honest Home.

D. C. And you think this a just and laudable Undertaking?

Woman. It cannot be otherwise, since it is only to keep him honest.

D. C. So you would send the Devil to your Husband, to prevent his going to a Whore, and all this for a bare Supposition only, for I cannot see you have any Ground to believe him false; and, if I may be allowed to know any thing of the Matter, there never was a better-natured, and more honest Man in the World; you are happy, if you know when you are so; therefore, instead of tormenting him, leave off your

Jealousy,

Jealoufy, and ill Humour, and be affable and obliging, as it is the Duty of a Wife to be, and, I will engage, you will have no Caufe of Complaint from him.

Woman. You tell me this only to fave yourfelf the Trouble of conjuring up a Spirit, but if you will not do it, I fhall go to thofe who will; I know there are them that will oblige me, and I fhould not be ungrateful.

D. C. If fuch a Thing were to be done, I had much rather it fhould be effected by any-body than myfelf; but, take my Word, whoever pretends to it, will but deceive you;--- I tell you once again, your Hufband is innocent, and you harbour a Fiend in your own Breaft, worfe than any you will ever procure to torment him: Jealoufy is the worft of Devils, and where it is caufelefs, brings its own Punifhment along with it.

Woman. And are you certain no Woman has any Share in his Affections but myfelf?

D. C. I dare anfwer for it.

Woman. I see, now, you are no better than an Impoftor; for I will fwear he faid, my Next-Door Neighbour's Wife, who is counted no better than fhe fhould be, was a very comely, agreeable Woman; I know he has a Defign upon her, and if you will not do as I have defired, I will go to all the Conjurers in *England,* but I will find one that fhall.

I used

I USED all the Arguments I was Master of, to perfuade this wicked Wretch to better Thoughts, but it was throwing Pearls before Swine; the more I urged, the more outrageous she grew, and, at laft, told me, *She believed I knew the Rogue her Hufband, and was his Confederate in abufing her.* In fhort, I was forced to take her by the Shoulder, and put her out of the Houfe, that her Noife might not difturb fome Ladies of Condition I had above.

IT would be endlefs to recount the Numbers that, thro' me, defired the Affiftance of the Devil to compafs their Defires; but as fome are too grofs for Repetition, and others too trifling, I fhall content myfelf with having given a Sample to what a Degree of Degeneracy humane Nature may fink, if not kept up by Religion, and good Senfe; for Wickednefs and Folly commonly go Hand in Hand.

CHAP.

CHAP. XV.

A Remarkable Instance of INGRATITUDE.

THO' I have already made Mention of my sincere Intentions of being serviceable to those who consulted me on any honest or legal Score, and the unkind Returns I sometimes have met with; yet I cannot resolve to lay down my Pen without relating one little History of an Affair transacted between me and a Person, who, I dare say, will count over many happy Years when I am Dust and Ashes. The Adventure is this.

Having made an Appointment with some Friends to meet at a Tavern, at a certain Hour, neither the Persuasions of my Wife, nor the Impatience of several Clients, who happened at that Time to be in the House, could prevent my keeping my Word, and, as I was breaking from them all, and had just set my Foot on the Stairs, I was saluted by a grave, old Gentleman in a plain Habit; the Sight of him had more Effect upon me, than all that had been alledged for my staying at Home, and I was compelled, as it were, by an inward Impulse to turn back, and
know

know his Business. I followed him into the Dining-Room, and presenting him a Pen and Ink, he immediately wrote in this Manner.

SIR, I have heard great Talk of you ——— My Life was once in great Danger ; let me know in what kind. I desire no other Proof of your Skill.

He gave me his Gold with his Question, and seemed impatient for my Answer, which I was not long before I obliged him with in these Terms.

SIR, You are a Gentleman who have not seen your native Land for thirty Years or upwards, and having been Witness of all the Rarities of the Globe, are curious of knowing whether you may reckon the Dumb Man *among the Number. As to the Danger of your Life, you had the Misfortune of being Poisoned by the Bite of a* Viper, *and was cured by a Wizard ——— You have no mortal Wounds, but wear Scars preferrable to a Star and Garter ——— I look on you as the Wonder of Mankind, the Glory of your illustrious Family in particular, and the Honour of your Country in general ——— You have fought both by Sea and Land, met with Storms, Tempests, and unequal Forces, yet never knew what it was to fear.*

The Gentleman had no sooner read this, than he pulled a green Purse out of his Pocket, in which

which was a large Gold Medal set round with Diamonds, and having shewn it me, wrote,

LET this convince you of the Truth of your Skill, as well as of my Honour, what you say is Fact; I was bit by a Viper, *which must have been my Death according to all humane Probability; for in five Minutes my Leg was swelled bigger than my Body, but by the Advice of some Friends, I sent for a famous* Wizard, *who, by uttering some mystical Words, immediately cured me.*

AFTER this we had a Bottle of Wine, and while we were drinking it, I had Leisure to examine the Lines of his Face more particularly, and seeing something which promised great Things, I wrote to him in these Terms.

I LOOK on you with Pleasure: You have nothing of the Rudeness which one might expect from a Person who has past so much Time among Infidels--- You have acquired all their Knowledge, but left their Barbarism behind you———You have a good Angel which constantly attends you——preserves you amidst the most imminent Dangers----but yet you must permit me to reproach you with Cowardice in one Thing———you have Twenty thousand Pounds yours Due from some great Powers, yet you have not Courage to demand it——— Methinks, all that can threaten such an Attempt is a Trifle to what you have undergone——— You have a very good Chance for getting it, but were there a thousand to one against you,

in

in Honour you ought not to relinquish tamely what is so much your Right———*If my Advice may prevail, be bold in the Affair*———*You will, I know, meet with some Repulses, but I dare assure you of Success in the End.*

I OBSERVED he paused, and seemed divided within himself when he read this, but gave me no direct Answer, and the Conversation between us took a different Turn. He came, however, almost every Day to visit me, and took an infinite Pleasure in being a Witness of the various Humours of my Consulters; and by what he saw me do in little Things, grew more convinced of my Abilities in great Ones; and when we had been acquainted about a Month, he wrote to me in the following Manner.

I am enough assured it is in your Power to effect every Thing that is in the Power of a Mortal, and would have you make your own Fortune, as well as that of other People.

To which I answered, *That I never had it in my Power to do myself much Service* ——— I had no sooner wrote this than he immediately resumed;

BUT, Mr. Campbel, *you are afflicted with Sickness, and acting in so publick a Manner as you do, must needs have drawn on you many Enemies*———*I am no Stranger to the Struggles you have*

have to defend yourself against the Barbarity of some People, and that it is not getting Five hundred Pounds per Ann. can preserve you from Ruin, while the Power and Malice of those who labour for your Undoing continue in the same Vigour. I have been thinking on the Twenty thousand Pounds you talked of; it is undoubtedly my Due, and if you will come to an Agreement with me, I will give you one Shilling in the Pound for as many Pounds as I shall recover.

I PRESENTLY told him, I would enter into any Measures which should be for his Good and my own; and he pursued his Discourse in this Manner;

IN the first Place, you must give me your Advice how to proceed; and next, you must take a Trip to Holland: For this last Article I will make you a Present of Two hundred Pounds, whether I get any Thing or not; but if I receive the Money, either the whole Sum, or Part, you shall be paid in Proportion; that is, according to what I offered before, one Shilling in the Pound.

I MADE a little Demur at going to *Holland*, because I knew that I should lose more by quitting my Business for so long a Time, besides the Vexation it would give my Clients. But on his telling me, he would desire my Company but six Weeks, I at last agreed, and a Lawyer being sent for, the Writings were drawn, One hundred

hundred Pounds was to be paid me down, and the other I was to receive as soon as I set Foot in *Holland.*

EVERY Thing being thus settled, I began to provide myself with traveling Garments, but all on a sudden I found my Friend grow cold ; he told me, *That he could not lay down any Money till our Arrival in* Holland, *and that he would have me embark before him, and go directly to* Rotterdam (*where he would follow me in a few Days.* This a little vexed me ; but though I was dissuaded by several of my Friends from proceeding in this Expedition, yet, as my Honour was engaged, I resolved to go through with it, and accordingly did, with a few Guineas in my Pocket, which he had given me for Earnest, and a Bill on a Dealer in *Rotterdam.*

WHAT I endured in this Voyage would be too tedious to recite, so I shall only say, that I had my Labour for my Pains, or, according to a silly Custom in Fashion among the Vulgar, was made an *April-Fool* of, the Person who had engaged me to take this Pains never meeting me, but, instead of keeping his Appointment, went strait to *Amsterdam*, and, according to the Advice I had given him, sollicited his Affair, and got Ten thousand Pounds paid in a short Time, out of which I never received one Farthing, nor have seen or heard from him since; but an Acquaintance of mine, who happened to be be his alfo, having fome Bufinefs in *Holland* met him by Chance, and afked him, *How he could be fo ungenerous as to fend me to* Rotterdam, *when he went to* Amfterdam; to which he gave this malicious Anfwer, *That Mr.* Campbel*'s Genius could have informed him where the Perfon was he came to meet, much better than any Direction.* I believe there is no-body but what will think this Evafion highly bafe; nor can it be fuppofed, but that I, who had been able to tell him fuch particular Things, which he owned were known to no Perfon in *England,* and had directed him by what Means he fhould recover his Money, could eafily have foretold, that I fhould be deceived by the very Perfon I took fo much Pains to ferve, had I endeavoured it; but I was too much taken up with other Studies to lay out any Part of my Time on an Affair in which I had no Sufpicion, and only thought of ferving him, while I fhould have thought how he intended to ferve me. Befides, my Agreement and Orders were to go to *Rotterdam:* I performed my Promife, and it was his Bufinefs to meet me, not mine to go in Search of him. But let his own Rod lafh him; the Ungrateful, fooner or later, may find one more ungrateful than themfelves, and are punifhed by the very Crime they have been guilty of---For my Part, tho' I ftill have the Articles of Agreement by me, and could prefently put them in Force, yet I fcorn to do it, leaving him to thofe fecret Stings which he cannot fail to feel, whenever Reflection fets what I have done for him before his Eyes.

The

The CONCLUSION.

IF there be any thing in this little Treatise which will oblige the Reader, and particularly my fair Consulters, the Glory of it will perpetuate my Memory: I assure them, none has had, and will to the last Moment of my Life continue to have, their Interest more at Heart; and, as I was always an Enemy to Flattery, cannot be suspected to be guilty of it in a Work which is not to see the Light till after my Decease; what is contained in it, will, doubtless, gain Belief, and, for that Reason, I am as certain, will be for the Advantage of those whose Good I shall never cease to wish living and dying.

THERE having been formerly-published a little Pamphlet, entitled, The *Friendly* DÆMON, but, I believe, is now very scarce; I have ordered it to be re-printed with this, because, in the Chapter of the *Loadstone*, I have omitted some Things which are contained in that, as also some genuine Letters from my Correspondents.

I HAVE no other Apology to make for the foregoing Pages, but that they are well meant, for which Reason I flatter myself they will be well taken, especially by my fair Consulters, this being the last Legacy from him they have been pleased to call *their Dumb Oracle*.

THE
Friendly Dæmon:
OR THE
Generous APPARITION.

To my anonymous worthy Friend, Physician, and Philosopher, whose Name, for certain Reasons, I forbear to mention.

SIR,

I CANNOT, without great Ingratitude, forget the friendly Visits, and kind Advice, I frequently received from you, during, not only a dangerous but tedious Indisposition, which surprizingly seized me in the Year 1717, and, notwithstanding your extraordinary Care, as well as unquestionable Judgment, continued on me till the latter-End of the Year --25; in which

which long Interval of Time, the Attendance you gave, and the Trouble you gave yourself, abstracted from all Interest, made you truly sensible of my unhappy Condition, and myself equally apprehensive of the great Obligations I shall ever be under to so sincere a Friend.

The first Occasion of my Illness, as I have good Reason to imagine, was a very shocking Surprize, given me by certain Persons, who pretended to be my Friends in a considerable Affair then depending, wherein their Treachery threatened me with succeeding Ruin, had not Providence interposed, and delivered the Oppressed from the cruel Hands of such deceitful Enemies: Upon whose hard Usage, and the News of my Disappointment, I was struck, at first, with a kind of Epilepsy, and deprived of all my Senses in an Instant, dropped down in the publick Coffee-House, under violent Agitations, which, it seems, are generally concomitant with this miserable Distemper; but being luckily assisted, and kindly supported by some Gentlemen present, I happened to escape those ill Consequences that might, otherwise, have attended me, during the Extremity of my Convulsions, which were reported, by those that held me, to be so strong, as to be almost insupportable, till the Paroxism declined, which terminated in a cold Sweat, Trembling, and Weeping, and this was the first Attack that ever this terrible Assailant made upon me; tho', afterwards, he forced himself into a further Familiarity with me (much against my Will) nor could your kind Endeavours, by the Art of Physick, backed with my own Strength of Constitution, fright away this evil Companion from me, till my good *Genius*, by the Direction of Providence, communicated a particular Secret to me, which, with God's Blessing, has lately proved my Deliverance, in what Manner, before I conclude, I shall very freely acquaint you, in Hopes you will favour me with your candid Opinion in Answer thereunto.

NEAR eight Years was a long Time to continue under the frequent Returns, and uncomfortable Dread of such a shocking Affliction, which, upon every little Disorder of Mind, or Disappointment in Business, never failed to visit me; till, by convulsive, or other involuntary Motions in my Head, and other Parts of my Body, my Eyes were buried in their Sockets; my other Features contracted; my Bowels sometimes wrack'd with intolerable Pains, and all the Faculties of my Mind so greatly weakened and impaired, that I, who, for many Years before, had been esteemed as an Oracle by the most polite and curious Part of both Sexes, was now, for want of Strength of Mind, and Ability of Body to imploy my Talent, and exercise my Art, as usual, treated like an old Soldier, who had lost his Limbs in the Service of his Country, and thought only worthy, by way of

Requital,

Requital, to be made a hobbling Pensioner in some starving Hospital; but, I thank my Stars, it proved not quite so bad with me, for tho' some Ladies were too hasty and importunate to bear with the least Disappointment, or admit of any Delay, without shewing their Resentment, or refusing to trust their Money till my Convulsions afforded me a rational Interval, wherein I might be able to give them ample Satisfaction: Yet, others, of a more considerate, easy and compassionate Temper, were so highly concerned for my too apparent Indisposition, that, in order to drive out this tormenting *Dæmon* that possessed me, they brought me all the old *Recipes* they could muster up among their crazy Aunts and Grandmothers, practised upon all Occasions in their several Families, perhaps ever since the Time of *Galen* and *Hippocrates*; but, having been long under the Care and Friendship of so able a Physician as yourself, tho' to little or no Purpose, I could not put Faith enough in old Women's Medicines to receive Benefit thereby; so, under a kind of Despondency of every thing but Providence, I suffered my Distemper to take its own Course, till my Fits increased upon me to at least twenty in a Day, and by their frequent Reiterations, brought, at length, such a Dimness upon my Sight, such a Weakness in my Joints, and Tremor upon my Nerves, that rendered me incapable of all manner of Business, especially that which I had so long professed, and successfully performed, to the full Satisfaction and great Aftonishment of Thousands; but being now unable to write, and, for want of Speech, having no other Way of communicating my Answers to the Demands of the Ladies and Gentlemen that applied themselves to me, except by Digitation, which they understood not, I was forced, sometimes, when much disordered by my Convulsions, to send them away dissatisfied, which, if it were any Mortification to them, proved a much greater to myself, because, upon my ready Performances in the Mystery I am Master of, depends the Welfare of my whole Family.

UNDER these unhappy Circumstances I laboured till the Month of *October*, in the Year --24, confined, by my Distemper, to my own Habitation, not daring to go Abroad, for Fear of falling in the Streets, having been surprized by my Fits in St. *James*'s Park, and several other Places; but, about this Time, being possessed with a strong Inclination to the *Cold-Bath*, near Sir *John Oldcastle*'s, and the great Desire I had to experience the same, being highly encouraged by your Advice and Approbation, I summoned all the Strength I had to my Assistance, and, pursuant to the Dictates of my own restless Mind, had Recourse thither accordingly, attended by a proper Person to take due Care of me, for fear of the worst.

I HAD not repeated this cold Expedient above twice or thrice, but I was senſible of the Benefits I received thereby, for my Diſtemper began to treat me with leſs Severity than uſual, and my Fits were ſuccceded with a greater Defluxion of Tears than what was common before I applied myſelf to the Bath; ſo that, after my Weeping was over, I found myſelf much refreſhed, and all my Faculties abundantly more alert, than at any Time they had been ſince my firſt Illneſs, inſomuch, that, from a timely Continuance of this external Application, I entertained great Hopes of a perfect Recovery; but, notwithſtanding my diligent Proſecution of this ſharp and ſhivering Method, I was, to my great Sorrow, unhappily diſapppointed; for my Convulſions were as frequent, tho' not ſo violent, as formerly, and I was now again diveſted of all Hopes of Relief, except by the Hand of Providence, having nothing to truſt to, but that infallible Phyſician who can cure all Things in an Inſtant.

THE Deſpondency I was now under of any Aſſiſtance from humane Art, and the ſlender Opinion you ſeemed to entertain of my Recovery, made my Intervals as melancholly as my Fits were troubleſome; oppreſſed with theſe hard Circumſtances, I ſupported a burthenſome Life, and dragg'd on the tedious Hours till the latter-end of the Year --25, about which Time, as I was ſlumbering one Morning in my Bed, after a restless Night, my good *Genius*, or Guardian-Angel, cloathed in a white Surplice, like a Singing-Boy, appeared before me, holding a Scrowl, or Label, in his Right-Hand, whereon the following Words were wrote in large Capitals.

READ, BELIEVE, AND PRACTISE; THE LOADSTONE SHALL BE YOUR CURE, WITH AN ADDITION OF THE POWDER HERE PRESCRIBED YOU; BUT KEEP THE LAST AS A SECRET, FOR WITH THAT AND THE MAGNET YOU SHALL RELIEVE NUMBERS IN DISTRESS, AND LIVE TO DO GREATER WONDERS THAN YOU HAVE HITHERTO PERFORMED; THEREFORE BE OF GOOD CHEAR, FOR YOU HAVE A FRIEND UNKNOWN, WHO, IN THE TIME OF TROUBLE, WILL NEVER FAIL YOU.

This comfortable News, tho' delivered to me after so surprizing a Manner, yet was it very welcome to a languishing Person, under a Complication of Misfortunes, notwithstanding, I had a great Struggle with my natural Reason, before I could convince myself of what I was yet confident my very Eyes had seen, or, at least, had been represented to me after an extraordinary Manner, for betwixt really seeing a Vision, or verily believing we do see it, there is but a slender Difference; however, the intire Confidence I had put in Providence, and the great Desire I had to
be

be relieved, were to me convincing Arguments, beyond all Objection, that my Guardian-Angel had actually appeared, and communicated to my Eyes the very Scrowl that I had read, the Words of which, left my Memory should have proved treacherous, I entered in my Pocket-Book, as they are before recited, the *Recipe* only excepted.

HAVING thus subjected my Reason to my Senses, or, at least, my Faith, for I either saw, or believed I saw, what I have here reported, I had nothing else to do, but to put in Practice the Receipt which my good *Genius* had imparted to me, tho' how to come at a *Loadstone*, seemed to me as difficult as to find out the Philosopher's Stone, having but a slender Knowledge of the Thing itself, and much less of its Virtues; however, upon Enquiry, I soon found out a certain Virtuoso, near *Moorfields*, who is an eminent Dealer in such sort of Curiosities, and, by his Assistance, I presently furnished myself with what I wanted, and sending for some fat Amber, and a certain Preparation of Steel, which I privately dispensed in a very particular Manner, according to the *Recipe* communicated by my *Genius*; then applying both as directed, was miraculously delivered, in a great measure, from those wracking Convulsions which had so long afflicted me, and, in less than a Month's Time, my whole Microcosm was restored to such a happy State of Health, Strength and Vivacity, that, Heaven be praised, I could do any Thing as usual, but,

if

if I leave off my *Loadstone* for two or three Days, which I have sometimes done, meerly out of Curiosity, my Fits, as yet, will remind me of my foolish Presumption, and force me to have Recourse to my wonderful Preservative, which has not only proved so great a Friend to myself, but has relieved others in the like Distress, and, as I have found by three or four late Experiments, is as effectual in suppressing Vapours, and removing or preventing Hysterick Fits in Women, as it is in Epilepsies and Convulsions in our own Sex, either Men or Children.

Now, Doctor, since I have happily conquer'd so stubborn an Enemy, by such miraculous Means as do not fail to assist others as well as myself, I desire you will vouchsafe me your real Sentiments of this uncommon Way of Cure, your Notions of the *Genii*, and the wonderful Manner of commucating the *Recipe* ; your Thoughts of the *Loadstone* and the Virtues thereof ; your Opinion of *Sympathy*, and the Cures performed thereby, for I know you are a Philosopher sufficient, as well as Physician, to give a very good Light into all these Mysteries, in which I own I am to seek ; therefore hope you will condescend so far as to spend a leisure Hour upon the foregoing Particulars, and you will infinitely oblige, *SIR*,

Your assured Friend,
and humble Servant,

DUNCAN CAMPBEL

To my Deaf and Dumb Friend, Mr. DUNCAN CAMPBEL, *in Anſwer to his Letter to an anonymous worthy Friend, Phyſician and Philoſopher.*

SIR,

I RECEIVED your Letter, and read the ſame with no leſs Surprize than Satisfaction; for, as I am greatly pleaſed at your miraculous Recovery, ſo I am equally aſtoniſhed at the wonderful Means by which it was obtained: I confeſs, I have been too great a Student in Phyſick and Natural Philoſophy, to entertain any extraordinary Opinion of Miracles, no ways accountable to humane Reaſon, except thoſe that concern Religion, which are brought down to our Knowledge well atteſted, and recommended to our Faith by unexceptionable Authorities; not but that I am ready to admit, *That the Power of Healing is in the Hand of Providence, and that ſome Patients, when their Diſtempers, through the Frailty of humane Judgment, derive their Eſſence from ſo obſcure an Original that even puzzles the Phyſician:* Then, I ſay, I am ſo free to acknowledge, when the Bleſſing of God accompanies the Adminiſtration, *That the moſt trifling Application*

in

in the Eyes of Art, may recover such Persons from the most dangerous Infirmities. This I look upon to be your extraordinary Case, and therefore think not the Means to which you ascribe your Cure, or the Manner of the *Recipe*'s being communicated to you, a proper Subject for a Physical Enquiry, unless you had sent me the Prescription of your *Genius*, which I understand by your Letter, you are obliged to conceal, and then, perhaps, I should have been able to have judged, in some Measure, which of the Applications are most essential, the *Powder* or the *Loadstone*; also, how far your *Guardian Angel* is a Regular Proficient in the modern Practice of Physick.

However, as you desire my Opinion of the *Genii*, the *Loadstone*, the *Powder of Sympathy*, and the like; I shall not be only willing to give you my own Thoughts, but the Sentiments of others, before I take my Leave, who have made the foregoing Particulars their principal Studies; and are therefore better acquainted with the Nature of Spirits, than I pretend to be.

As for the *Genii* or familiar Spirits, good and bad, believed and reported, by the most Wise and Learned of the Ancients, to attend Mankind, and the various Operations they have had upon humane Minds as well as Bodies, I cannot but confess, seem very wonderful to my defective Understanding; yet, when we observe what innumerable Instances have been handed to us by

the

the most reputable Authors, both Ancient and Modern, attested from Time to Time by unquestionable Authorities, who, that, before he dived into these Mysteries, looked upon the same to be Whimsy, can forbear staggering in his Opinion?

THE most celebrated Instance of a *Genius* among the Ancients, is that of *Socrates*, one of the wisest of the Philosophers in the Age he lived in, and that he had such a familiar Spirit to attend him, which the *Greeks* called *Dæmon*, and the *Latins*, *Genius*, is sufficiently testified by three of his Cotemporaries, *viz. Plato, Xenophon,* and *Antisthenes*; also further confirmed by *Laertius, Plutarch, Maximus Tyrius, Dion, Chrysostomus, Cicero, Apuleius,* and *Facinas*; besides others more Modern, as, *Tertullian, Origen, Clemens Alexandrinus,* &c. but that which is of greater Authority than all the Vouchers aforementioned, is what *Socrates* says of himself, in *Plato's Theage*, viz. *By some divine Lot, I have a certain* Dæmon, *which has followed me from my Childhood, as an Oracle*; *and this Voice,* says he, for so he terms it, *whenever it speaks to me, dissuades me from engaging in what I am about to put in Action, but never prompts me to attempt any thing.* This, I presume, might be the chief Reason why *Socrates* pursued not his own Inclinations, which were naturally Vicious, as himself confessed to the Physiognomist, but was always accompanied with a divine Spirit that restrained him from it; for, in speaking to *Alcibiades*, a vicious Nobleman of *Athens*, but reclaimed by *Socrates*, says he, *My Tutor* (meaning the Spirit that attended him) *is wiser and better than you.* And to shew further, that what he called his *Dæmon* was something more than a secret Impulse of the Mind, or Dictates of a good Conscience, *Theocritus* affirms in *Plutarch, That a Vision attended* Socrates *from his Childhood, going before him, and guiding him in all the Actions of his Life, being a constant Light to him in such Affairs as lay not within the Reach of human Understanding, and that the Spirit often spoke to him, divinely governing and inspiring his Intentions.* A thousand Instances of the like Nature, I could collect from the Ancients, to prove, that what you have reported to me, in your Letter, may be no Delusion, but real Fact, with all its surprising Circumstances, could the Task be comprised within the Compass of a Letter, but, a Treatise of this Nature, being much fitter for a Volume, I shall only proceed to a few familiar Instances of a more modern Date, that your wonderful Cure may gain Credit with the Publick, because I know your Sincerity.

FROISSARD reports, That in the Time of *Edward* III. there was a certain Knight in *France*, called *Corasse*, who could tell every Thing transacted throughout the whole World, in a Day or two at the most, were the Distance never so remote; and this he did by an invisible
In-

Intelligencer or familiar Spirit, which he called *Orthone*, who was always at his Command, and brought him News continually for many Years, till, at laſt, he loſt the Benefit of ſo uſeful a Companion, through a vain Deſire of gratifying his Curioſity after the following Manner, *viz.* The Knight, having hitherto only heard the Voice of his ſpiritual Emiſſary, was now infatuated with an earneſt Inclination to behold his Shape, which Favour he requeſted of *Orthone*; accordingly, whoſe Anſwer was, *That the firſt Thing he ſhould ſee on the Morrow Morning, after he was riſen from his Bed, ſhould be the Object he deſired,* or Words to that Effect. The Knight, the next Morning, purſuant to the Direction of the Spirit, aroſe from his Bed, looked about him, but could not diſcover any Thing worthy of Remark; upon which Diſappointment, he upbraided *Orthone* with being worſe than his Word; who replied, *He had kept his Promiſe, deſiring the Knight to remind himſelf of what he had firſt obſerved after his Riſing*; the Knight, upon Recollection, replied, *That he ſaw nothing uncommon, but a Couple of Straws tumbling upon the Ground, and ſporting one with another; as if agitated by the Wind*; *That was I*, ſaith the Spirit, *and therefore I kept my Word*. Then the Knight deſired *to ſee him once more, in ſuch a Shape as might induce him, the next Time, to take more Notice of him*; to which the Spirit conſented, ſaying, *The firſt Thing you ſee on the morrow Morning, after your up-riſing, ſhall be me again*: Accordingly, when the Time appointed was come, and the Knight risen from his Bed, looking out of his Chamber-Window, the first Object he espied, was a lean, ill-favour'd Sow, so deformed and ugly, that he was not able to abide the Sight of her; and not expecting *Orthone* to appear to him in so homely a Manner, he set his Dogs upon the Sow to drive her away, who being highly affronted at such an unfriendly Usage, immediately vanished, to the Knight's great Surprize; and his old Acquaintance *Orthone* never came near him after. This Relation *Froissard* asserts he had from the Knight's own Mouth, with whom he was very intimate.

From hence I conclude, that the same Sort of Spirit that attended *Corasse*, has been always a Friend to you, not only of late, in your miraculous Recovery, but has at all Times assisted you in writing the Name of Strangers, discovering the most secret Intrigues, and foretelling future Events, for which you have been Famous. As for a further Proof of the Existence of Spirits, and that, at some other Times, as well as in your Case, they have prescribed Physick to their living Friends, I shall quote an Instance out of Mr. *Glanvil's Reports*, attested by the Lord *Orrery*, the Famous Mr. *Greatrix*, and many others, living in the Reign of King *Charles* the Second.

A

A Gentleman in *Ireland*, near to the Earl of *Orrery*'s House, sending his Butler one Afternoon to a neighbouring Village to buy Cards, as he passed a Field, espied a Company in the Middle thereof, sitting round a Table, with several Dishes of good Cheer before them, and moving towards them, they all rose and saluted him, desiring him to sit down and take Part with them; but one of them whispered these Words in his Ear, *viz. Do nothing this Company invites you to*: Whereupon, he refusing to except of their Kindness, the Table, and all the Dainties it was furnished with, immediately vanished, but the Company fell to Dancing and playing upon divers musical Instruments: The Butler was a second Time sollicited to partake of their Diversions, but would not be prevailed upon to engage himself with them; upon which, they left off their Merry-making and fell to Work, still pressing the Butler to make one among them, but to no Purpose; so that, upon his third Refusal, they all vanished and left the Butler alone, who, in a great Consternation, returned Home without the Cards, fell into a Fit as he entered the House, but soon recovering his Senses, related to his Master all that had passed.

The following Night, one of the Ghostly Company came to his Bed-Side, and told him, *That if he offered to stir out the next Day, he would be carried away*; upon whose Advice, he kept within till towards the Evening, and having Occasion to make Water, ventured to set one Foot over the Threshold of the Door, in order to ease himself, which he had no sooner done, but a Rope was cast about his Middle, in the Sight of several Standers-by, and the poor Man was hurried from the Porch with unaccountable Swiftness, followed by many Persons, but they were not nimble enough to overtake him, till a Horseman, well mounted, happening to meet him upon the Road, and seeing many Followers in pursuit of a Man hurried along in a Rope, without any-body to force him, catched hold of the Cord and stopped him in his Career, but received, for his Pains, such a Strap upon his Back with one End of the Rope, as almost felled him from his Horse; however, being a good Christian, he was too strong for the Devil, and recovered the Butler out of the Spirits Clutches, and brought him back to his Friends.

THE Lord *Orrery*, hearing of these strange Passages, for his further Satisfaction of the Truth thereof, sent for the Butler, with Leave of his Master, to come and continue some Days and Nights at his House, which, in Obedience to his Lordship, the Servant did accordingly, who, after his first Night's Bedding there, reported to the Earl in the Morning, *That his Spectre had again been with him, and assured him, that on that very Day he should be spirited away, in Spight of all the Measures that could possibly be taken to prevent it.*

it. Upon which he was conducted into a large Room, with a confiderable Number of holy Perfons to defend him from the Affaults of Satan; among whom was the famous Stroker of betwitched Perfon, Mr. *Greatrix*, who lived in the Neighbourhood, and knew, as may be prefumed, how to deal with the Devil as well as any-body; befides feveral eminent Quality were prefent in the Houfe, among the reft, two Bifhops, all waiting the wonderful Event of this unaccountable Prodigy.

TILL part of the Afternoon was fpent, the Time flid away in nothing but Peace and Quietnefs, but, at length, the enchanted Patient was perceived to rife from the Floor without any vifible Affiftance, whereupon Mr. *Greatrix*, and another lufty Man, clapt their Arms over his Shoulders, and endeavoured to weigh him down with their utmoft Strength, but to no Purpofe, for the Devil proved too powerful, and, after a hard Struggle on both Sides, made them quit their Hold, and fnatching the Butler from them, carried him over their Heads and toffed him in the Air, to and fro, like a Dog in a Blanket; feveral of the Company running under the poor Wretch to fave him from the Ground, by which Means, when the Spirits Frolick was over, they could not find that in all this Hurryfcurry, the frighted Butler had received the leaft Damage, but was left in *Statu quo*, upon the fame Premifes, to prove the Devil a Liar.

THE Goblins, for this Bout, having given over their Paſtime, and left their May-game to take a little Repoſe, that he might in ſome Meaſure be refreſhed againſt their next Sally, my Lord ordered, the ſame Night, two of his Servants to lie with him, for fear ſome Devil or other ſhould come and catch him napping, notwithſtanding which, the Butler told his Lordſhip the next Morning, *That the Spirit had again been with him in the Likeneſs of a Quack Doctor, and held in his Right-Hand a wooden Diſh full of grey Liquor, like a Meſs of Porridge,* at the Sight of which he endeavoured to awake his Bedfellows, but the Spectre told him, his Attempts were fruitleſs, for that his Companions were enchanted into a deep Sleep, adviſing him not to be frighted, for he came as a Friend, and was the ſame Spirit that cautioned him in the Field againſt complying with the Company he there met, when he was going for the Cards; adding, *That if he had not refuſed to come into their Meaſures, he had been for ever miſerable;* alſo wondered he had eſcaped the Day before, becauſe he knew there was ſo powerful a Combination againſt him; that for the future there would be no more Attempts of the like Nature; further telling the poor trembling Butler, *That he knew he was ſadly troubled with two Sorts of Fits,* and, therefore, as a Friend, he had brought him a Medicine that would cure him of both, beſeeching him to take it; but the poor Patient, who had been ſcurvily uſed by theſe Sort of Doctors, and fearing the Devil might be at

the

the Bottom of the Cup, would not be prevailed upon to swallow the Dose, which made the Spirit angry; who told him, however, *He had a Kindness for him, and that if he would bruise the Roots of* Plantane *without the Leaves, and drink the Juice thereof, it should certainly cure him of one Sort of his Fits, but as a Punishment for his Obstinacy in refusing the Liquor, he should carry the other with him to his Grave;* then the spiritual Doctor asked his Patient *if he knew him;* the Butler answered, *No*; I am, says he, *the wandering Ghost of your old Acquaintance* John Hobby, *who has been dead and buried these seven Years; and ever since, for the Wickedness of my Life, have been lifted into the Company of those evil Spirits you beheld in the Fields, am hurried up and down in this restless Condition, and doomed to continue in the same wretched State till the Day of Judgment.* Adding, That *had you served your Creator in the Days of your Youth, and offered up your Prayers that Morning before you were sent for the Cards, you had not been treated by the Spirits that tormented you, with so much Rigour and Severity.*

AFTER the Butler had reported these marvellous Passages to my Lord and his Family, the two Bishops, that were present, among other Quality, were thereupon consulted, *whether or no it was proper for the Butler to follow the Spirit's Advice, in taking the Plantane Juice for the Cure of his Fits, and whether he had done well or ill, in refusing the liquid Dose which the Spectre would*

would have given him: The Question, at first, seemed to be a kind of moot Point, but, after some Struggle in the Debate, their Resolution was, *That the Butler had acted, thro' the whole Affair, like a good Christian, for that it was highly sinful to follow the Devil's Advice in any Thing, and that no Man should do Evil that Good might come of it*; so that, in short, the poor Butler, after his Fatigue, had no Amends for his Trouble, but was denied, by the Bishops, the seeming Benefit that the Spirit intended him.

I do not introduce this old surprising Story to amuse you, but to let you know, that it is no new Thing for Spectres to turn Doctors to ailing Persons as they retain a Respect for, and that your *Genius* was not the first Spirit that ever practised Physick; therefore, if this Narrative, reported by *Glanvil*, *Beaumont*, and others, may obtain Credit, upon the Authorities of my Lord *Orrery*, Mr. *Greatrix*, and divers Persons, who were in a great Measure Eye-witnesses of the Matter, I see no Reason I have to doubt the Truth of your Letter, since I know your Integrity; besides, has always been allowed by such Dæmonologers as have published their Thoughts upon the Visibility of Spirits, that *Scotland* is never without such a Sort of People as they call *Second-sighted*, who have not only the Power of discerning Apparitions, but, by their frequent Conversation with Spirits, foretel future Events, to the great Astonishment of all Persons that

con-

consult them: That there are such a Sort of Diviners in the World, especially in *Scotland*, I am throughly convinced; of which Number I take yourself to be one, but how to account for your mysterious Performances, I readily confess, I know not, and therefore shall submit that Task to such as are qualified with a more subtil Penetration.

I DOUBT I have tired your Patience with too much Prolixity upon familiar Spirits, therefore, to make you amends, I will be but short in my Dissertation upon the *Loadstone*; which, in the first Place, is a very ponderous *Fossile*, found in different Climates, and seems in its Nature and Qualities to be nearly related to *Iron Oar*, from whence it is endowed with a peculiar Property of drawing to itself by the Power of Sympathy, or the natural Disposition it has to embrace that particular Metal. In *Ægypt* there are large Mines of it, some few Magnets have been found in *Æthiopia*, which have attracted *Iron* very forcibly; but two Sorts are dug up at the Foot of the *Sardinian* Mountains, of such different Natures, that as one *draws Iron*, the other will *repel it*; as you will find it reported by *Johannes Jonstonus*, in his History of *Nature*; also by *Pliny*, in his Second Book, who, for the aforesaid Reason, calls this Stone *Theamedes*: As to the singular Virtues hitherto discovered in the *common Loadstone*, the most admirable of all are the strict Correspondence it maintains with the

the two Poles, and the wonderful Property it communicates by a Touch to the Needle, for the Benefit of Mariners. The Power of its Attraction is thought by some Virtuosos to be owing to a clammy bituminous Substance, by which the Contexture of the more solid Parts are closely femented and confirmed; to prove this, work a *Loadstone* in the Fire and it shall cast forth a bluish Flame, like that of lighted Brimstone, and so continue till it spends its Life, and loses the Power of Attraction. There is a great deal of *Sulphur* in *Iron* as well as in the *Loadstone*; which is the principal Cause of their Sympathising with each other, and if you destroy the First in either, the last will fail in course, which is the Reason why the *Loadstone* will not attract the *Rust of Iron*, tho' it will the *Filings*, because in the former the bituminous Matter is quite spent, and nothing left but a kind of *Caput mortuum*. The *Loadstone* hath also two Poles, which answer those in the Heavens; if you touch the Needle with the *North Pole* of the Stone, it will point to the *Artick*, if with the *South* Part thereof, as it stood posited in the Mine, it will point to the *Antartick*, but not with the utmost Exactness, except it stands in the *Meridian:* But to be further satisfied in these Mysteries, have Recourse to *Libavious, Cardanus, Pliny, Bodin, Porta,* our own *Philosophical Transactions,* and such Authors as have treated more largely upon this Subject: For, I suppose, all that you want to know of me is, if ever I have heard from others, or discovered

covered by my own Experience, any such Physical Virtue in the *Loadstone*, as may tend to the Cure of any Chronical or other Disease incident to human Bodies, that may strengthen the Opinion you seem to entertain of it in such Cases, from the Benefit yourself has lately received in so extraordinary a Manner.

In answer to this, I confess, I have heard affirmed (but not by a Physician) *That the Loadstone hath withdrawn the Inflamation, and given Ease in the Gout, and by changing the Application of it from one Side to the other, has at length chased it away, to the perfect Recovery of the Patient*; but in any other Case, excepting your own, I never heard of a Cure so much as facilitated or attempted to be performed thereby; therefore, as the Use of it in any Disease is quite Foreign to the common Practice of Physick, if others, as well as yourself, have received Benefit by this new Discovery, I think not myself obliged to account for it, till it becomes practical among my own Fraternity, and then it will be time enough for any Physician to give his Thoughts thereon; besides, I am a Stranger to the Preparation prescribed to you by your *Genius*, and without the Knowledge of that material Secret, it is impossi- for any Physician, in your Case, to make a clear Judgment, or to know which of the two your Cure is chiefly owing to, the *Powder* or the *Loadstone*; for how far the latter may operate upon a Body prepared by *Pulvis Martis* or other *Chalybeates*, I shall not pretend to determine,

tho'

tho', for ought I know, wonderful Cures may be performed in that Way, but upon what Reafon in Nature, fuch a new Syftem can be founded, feems very remote from my prefent Underftanding; but, fince you are become fole Mafter of fo wonderful a Secret, my Advice is, *That you keep the* Recipe *to yourfelf, in Obedience to your* Genius, *and tho' you affift others, never do it without Fee or Reward, for all ufeful Difcoveries ought to be rendered Profitable.*

In anfwer to the laft Article of your Requeft, I fhall now proceed to fay fomething of *Sympathy*, and the Cures reported to have been done thereby. The *Sympathetick Powder*, fo highly efteemed about a hundred Years fince, by Men of Art in this Kingdom, was firft brought into *Europe* by a religious *Carmelite*, who, in his Travels thro' *India*, *Perfia*, and *China*, had made himfelf Mafter of this Secret, and from fome of thofe *Eaftern* Countries, came over into *Tufcany*, where he perform'd many confiderable Cures by this occult Method, to the great Aftonifhment of the moft eminent Phyficians and Surgeons in thofe Parts; infomuch that the Duke of *Tufcany* himfelf was very defirous of becoming Mafter of this furprizing *Arcanum*, but the honeft Fryar, by many handfome Excufes brought himfelf off, and would not be prevailed upon to communicate his *Noftrum* to his Highnefs.

SOME

SOME few Months after this, our famous *English* Virtuoso, Sir *Kenelm Digby*, happening, in his Travels, to be at the Grand Duke's Court, an Opportunity fell accidentally in the Knight's way to do the Fryar a Service, which the good old Man took so kindly at his Hands, that he recompenced the Curtesy with a Discovery of his Secret; and soon after returning into *Persia*, left no Man in *Europe* Master of the same but Sir *Kenelm*, who was the first Person that brought the *Recipe* into *England*, and that here wrought Cures by it himself, and reeommended it to the Practice of others; so that, in a little Time, every Mother-Midwife and Country Fleabeard, became topping Surgeons, especially for the Cure of Green Wounds; for it is not to be trusted to in other Cases.

THIS *Sympathetick Powder*, by which many Miracles have been performed at great Distances, is nothing more than the Simple Powder of *Roman Vitriol*, either chymically prepared, or imperfectly calcined in the Beams of the Sun; from whence, 'tis said, it derives a very balsamick Virtue: A little of this applied to any Instrument that has done Mischief, or to a Rag diped into, or stained with the Blood of a Wound, never fails of curing the Patient at the widest Distance, provided the Wound be curable.

Sir

Sir KENELM DIGBY, to advance the Credit of this surprising Medicine, speaks very largely in Commendation thereof, in a little Treatise of his, written first in *French*, upon the same Subject; wherein he boasts of a remarkable Cure performed by himself, in a most wonderful Manner, with only the Use of this astonishing Powder; and, therefore, as in religious Cases, Example goes beyond Precept, so, to convince you of the Miracles performed by Sympathy, Instances, perhaps, may prove more effectual than Arguments; for which Reason, I shall proceed to furnish you with a notable Experiment of this *Magical Powder*, and so conclude.

Mr. JAMES HOWEL, *a trusty Servant to King* James I. *famous in those Days for compiling a Treatise, entitled* Dendrologia, *and afterwards for his Legacy to the World, called,* Epistolæ Ho-Elianæ, *happened, when he was a young Gentleman, to accidentally come by, when two of his dearest Friends were fiercely engaged in a very dangerous Duel, and to prevent further Mischief, very likely to ensue, too rashly catched hold, with his naked Hand, of his Sword whose Passion prompted him to be the most desperate; in which Attempt, the Weapon being drawn through Mr.* Howel's *Palm, cut the Nerves and Muscles thereof to the very Bone, and, as they were thus Scuffling, holding up the same Hand to defend one of his Friends from a Blow upon his Head, received another Cut upon the Back of his Hand, cross*

all

all the Veins and Tendons, more terrible than the former, which, his Friends perceiving, put a sudden Stop to their inebrious Fury, run both to embrace him, and express their Sorrow for the unhappy Accident, lending him their Assistance to bind up his Wounds with his own Garters, and so conducted him to his Lodgings, where they sent directly for a Surgeon, who found the Case desperate, for he bled abundantly.

Mr. HOWEL being a Gentleman much respected by the Quality, the News of his Misfortune soon reached the Court; and his Majesty having a great Regard for him, sent one of his own Surgeons to attend him, who found the Case to be so very bad that he seemed doubtful of a Cure, without cutting off his Hand, which occasioned Mr. Howel, about five Days after the Hurt was received, to apply himself to his good Friend and Neighbour, Sir Kenelm Digby, who, at that time was famous for the Sympathetick-Powder, begging his Assistance in that painful Extremity, telling him, That his Surgeons were apprehensive of a Gangrene.

Sir KENELM, opening the Wounds, found a terrible Case of it, and a dangerous Inflamation upon the Part, which, Mr. Howel acknowledged, gave him such intolerable Pain as was scarce supportable: The Knight asked him, If he had any Bandage with the Blood upon it; Mr. Howel answered, Yes; accordingly sent his Servant for the bloody Garter which had first bound up his Wounds, and delivered it to Sir Kenelm, who, calling for a Bason of Water, went into his Closet for a Handful of his Powder, which he infused therein, and then soaked the Garter in the same Liquor; whilst Mr. Howel was talking with another Gentleman, at the further End of the Room, not knowing in the least what Sir Kenelm was doing, who, after he had bathed the Garter in the Bason about a Minute, called to his Patient, and asked him, How he found himself, who answered, So wonderful easy that the Inflamation seems to be totally extinguished, the Pain quite gone off, and my Hand I find as cool and as much refreshed as if it was wrapped up in a wet Napkin. Then, *replied the Knight*, fling off your Dressings, meddle no more with Plaisters, only keep your Wounds clean and from the Air, and I doubt not, but in a few Days Time, I shall effectually cure you, without putting you to any further Trouble. *Much comforted with this Assurance,* Mr. Howel *took a thankful Leave of Sir* Kenelm, *and so departed.*

Mr. Howel *had not been gone above a Quarter of an Hour, before the Knight took the Garter out of the Liquor, to dry it before the Fire, and carelesly hanging it a little too near, the extraordinary Heat, by the Concatination of Effluvia's, had such an Effect upon the Patient, that he made as many wry Faces as a Cook that had burnt his Fingers: upon which he dispatched his Servant, with all imaginable Expedition, to let his Doctor know what a Condition he was relapsed into.*

Sir

Sir KENELM, *who presently conjectured the Cause of this Disaster, smiling at the Message the Servant had delivered, aud snatching the Garter from the Fire, told him,* That his Master should be very easy by the Time he could return to him, *which the Footman, by the Acknowledgment of his Master, found to be true accordingly*; *Sir* Kenelm *doing nothing more to work this Change, than cooling the wreaking Garter by a speedy Repetition of his former Application*; *so that, without any further Accident interposing, the Patient was thoroughly cured, in five or six Days Time, by this extraordinary Method, to the inexpressible Admiration of all his Majesty's Surgeons.*

S I R, This is all, at present, I am at leisure to say in Answer to your Letter, and, I doubt, you will think it enough too, except more to the Purpose: What extraordinary Cures you happen to perform by your new Method, I desire you will communicate to me as soon as you can conveniently, for to hear of your Success, will be no little Satisfaction to,

S I R,

Your assured Friend,

and humble Servant,

ORIGINAL LETTERS

SENT TO

Mr. *Campbel* by his Confulters.

LETTER I.

From a Perfon under great Misfortunes.

SIR,

I AM much concerned at the Account you give me of your Indifpofition, and wifh Health and Wealth may join to make you eafy: As for myfelf, though I endeavour all I am able to follow your Prefcriptions in Patience, and Refignation to the Will of Heaven, yet, I confefs, the Tide of Misfortunes has almoft overwhelmed me, and it muft now be a ftrong and fudden Gale of good Fortune that can preferve me from finking in the Sea of Grief and Confufion.

I HAVE, dear Sir, neither so little Fortitude, nor so much Self-Love, as not to bear the utmost my cruel Stars, or the more cruel World, can inflict on me, were the Destruction wholly mine; but when I reflect that with my Ruin, that of so dear a Friend as C———n is blended; all that we can summon in such Tryals, is too weak to support me, and I am ready to call in Question that supreme Justice, which, as you piously remonstrate, is above all humane Comprehension.

I MUST own, there is something in the Consciousness of what has rendered that worthy Man unhappy by my ill Conduct and Inadvertency, that is more shocking than all the Tortures invented for corporeal Punishment, and I would rather chuse to go out of the World with my Heart broke with Sorrows, than to continue in it, and see him suffer for my sake.

BUT you assure me all will be well in Time, and that I shall yet taste of Happiness; You seem certain also, that the good Fortune yourself has long expected, is now near at Hand; I pray Heaven it may be so; I wish yours may shew mine the Way; and that nothing hereafter may ruffle a Mind in itself so full of Harmony, and so inclinable to heal the Wounds of others, and particularly of,

SIR,
Your very sincere and devoted Servant.

LETTER II.

From a Gentleman in the Country.

SIR,

YOU may remember when I was laft in Town, our Difcourfe turned chiefly on the Intelligence of the invifible World, and that I then afked your Opinion concerning an Intercourfe between the embodied Spirits of feparated Friends, to which you anfwered in the Negative, unlefs in Dreams or Vifions; I did not, at that Time, give you my Reafons for this Queftion, but being now confirmed in what I before conjectured, I will relate the whole Affair, and doubt not but it will afford you Matter of Speculation.

THE whole Time I continued in *London*, which I think was three Weeks and two Days, whatever Company I was in, or however employed, I could not put it out of my Head, that my Friend here had entertained a Chimera of my having left *Walton* for ever; I thought it highly unreafonable fhe fhould imagine fo, becaufe the Affair which firft brought me to this Part of the Country, being in the fame Situation it was, I fhould have little Regard for myfelf to leave it, and was expoftulating with her in my Mind on fo groundlefs a Sufpicion: But I had no fooner arrived, than a few Minutes Conference gave me

the

the Assurance of every Particular my Fancy had represented to me.

I must confess, this is a convincing Proof to me, that the Souls of absent Persons meet and inform each other of their respective Circumstances, Desires, and Passions; for to be free, though I never owned so much to any one before, I had an Inclination rather to make up my Affair at any Rate, than return to that mountainous Wild, where I live a savage Life, without any Thing of my own Specie to converse with, for I look on the Inhabitants of this Place as but a superior Degree of Brutes, and, indeed, what else can they be justly termed, whose Minds are neither cultivated by Learning or good Manners.

As it was therefore Necessity that drove me down, and I had so carefully concealed the Secret in my own Breast, what, but my tell-tale Spirit could betray it to her? Or what but her's reveal her Suspicion of it to me? I should be glad you would bestow a few Moments in Reflection of this abstruse Point, and communicate your deliberate Judgment on it to him, who must, in spight of himself, be for some Time longer a *Waltonian*, but always with his best Wishes,

Mr. Campbel's

Very humble Servant.

LETTER III.

From a Lady, who, from the Depth of Misery was suddenly raised to Happiness.

Dear SIR,

I Should be utterly unworthy the good Fortune which, next to Heaven, is entirely owing to the admirable *Talisman* I received from you, if I did not acknowledge it in a Manner suitable to the Obligation. The purest Sacrafice springs from the Heart, and you that have foreseen so much of me, as to give me Directions for Happiness, will, doubtless, see mine glows with the most perfect Gratitude.

It is now six Weeks since I have been married, and every Thing has happened in the very Manner you foretold. Mrs. B——, once my triumphant Rival, is now the Jest of the whole Country; despised by every-body; pitied by none; and my Spouse is so far from having the least Remains of Tenderness for her, that he even hates to hear her Name: As to my Law-Suit, it being tried in Town, I doubt not but you have already heard my good Success, but lest you should not, give me Leave to acquaint you, that I have recovered the Whole of what I sued for with Damages. We have sent to Town to bespeak a fine Chariot and Equipage, which, when

when finished, we shall be there ourselves; and you may depend on seeing me as frequently now I have no farther to follicite of you, as when my whole Hope lay on your Care and Skill.

But as Providence sometimes is pleased to disappoint our best Intentions, I beg, as an Earnest of my future Gratitude, you will accept of Fifty Pounds, which I have ordered Mr. H—— to pay you on the Sight of this; and believe, that while I have Life, nay, after, if what you say be true, that the Dead are allowed to hold Communication with the Living, I shall be ever,

Dear SIR,

Your most obliged

and sincere Friend.

LETTER IV.

From an old Correspondent.

Worthy SIR,

THO' I do nothing with greater Pleasure than writing to you, yet my Pen flows now with double Readiness, because it has an Opportunity of obliging you, and, at the same Time, a Friend, for whom we both have a very great Esteem.

EITHER

EITHER something very extraordinary has been the Occasion, or Mrs. S—— has gained the unexpected Character of being Rich; for on *Monday* Night last, when all the Family were in Bed, I was surprised with a Noise of a Pick-axe under my Window; I listened some time, and being convinced it was more than Imagination, rose, and called *James*, who was the only Man besides myself at that Time in the House; on searching, we found there was a Hole broke in the Wall, almost big enough for a Man to enter: Being so small a Posty, we judged it not safe to venture out, and therefore removed the best of the Goods into the inner Rooms, which we barricadoed as well as we could, then putting out the Candles, set ourselves to watch in my Chamber. Nothing happened till the Clock had struck Three, when we saw the Glimmering of a Lanthorn at the Breach I mentioned; on which I threw open the Window, and examined with a loaded Musquet, but unhappily missed the Person.

SHE has been ever since in very great Agitations, imagining this Attempt was not made by a Theif, but by her discarded Suiter Mr. D——, who, by his Threats and Deporture, gives, indeed, some Cause for this Suspicion. She has, however, removed her best Effects to the House of Mr. L——, who still continues his Addresses to her, but does not come directly to the Point: She

She therefore begs you would compose a Philter, if it may be done, to keep his Passion towards her up to the same Degree of Warmth in Absence, as it seems to be when she is present; and also, that you will consult your *Genius* for a certain Intelligence, whether the Person who attempted to break into the House, came with an Intent of robbing, or of murdering her, which latter she is assured of if it were really *D——*; we join in our Entreaties, that you will be as speedy and possitive as possible in your Reply, and that you will let us know if we have any farther Attacks to dread from the same Hand.

As you are so good to look more on the Intention than on the meer Value of an Offering, she sends you, with her best Respects, a couple of Turkeys, a Ham of her own Drying, and one Guinea, which is all her Ability allows at this Time. As for myself, you are so well convinced of what I would do, had I the Power, that it is utterly needless to add any more than that I am, as ever,

Your faithful Friend,
and humble Servant.

LET-

LETTER V.

From a Jew *residing at* Constantinople.

SIR,

GRATITUDE is ever the Token of a noble Soul, and among the many on whom, I bless God, it has been in my Power to confer Obligations, I have found few so ready to acknowledge them as yourself. It was, indeed, this Opinion of you, which made me first conceive so great an Esteem for you, and the Confirmation binds me eternally to your Service. But that I may not be found guilty of a Want of that in myself, which I am applauding in you, accept of my very hearty Thanks for your kind Present of the admirable *Invisible Ink*. I assure you, it is of the utmost Service to me among these Barbarians, as you will perceive when, by a fitter Opportunity, I write with it some Adventures which have lately befallen me here. The most perplexing of them I here give you a Hint on, for a Word to the Wise is enough. You may remember you bid me beware of Beauty, especially in the Forty-second Year of my Age; your own Familiar will inform you the rest, but if he should be employed on more material Affairs, you shall know it from myself in a short Time, with all the News of this City, that I think worthy your Attention; till then keep me in your Memory, and may the God of *Juda* be your Guide in all Things. I am, without Deceit,

Your most affectionate Friend.

LETTER VI.

From a Lady of Distinction.

Mr. CAMPBEL,

I WAS some Years ago with you, when you told me of a Misfortune I had just then passed over, aud predicted one I was in Danger of falling into about this Time; you did not mention of what Kind, but it being now arrived will inform you, and intreat your Advice in what Manner I shall proceed.

THE first Effect of my ill Stars was, to suffer me to fall under the Temptation of a certain Man of Quality, by whom I had a Son, but the Honour of my Lover, and my own Prudence, screened the Matter so well that it was never talked of, nor did my Husband, whom I married soon after, ever suspect any Thing had happened. I have since had many Children, the Eldest of whom is a Girl of uncommon Beauty, being now fifteen Years of Age. Who should the Malice of my Fate make sensible of her Charms but my own Son, who, unknowing he is so, addresses her for Marriage? She is no less pleased with him

him, and my Husband wholly satisfied with the Character and Fortune of the young Gentleman (his Father being dead, and having left him Twenty thousand Pounds) resolves it shall be a Match: All that I can say against it avails nothing, because I can assign no Reason which appears just. Help me, dear *Dumb Oracle*, in this Extremity; I tremble at the Thought of Incest, yet cannot resolve to unravel the Mistery. If you can any way find a Clue to guide me through this Labyrinth, the five Guineas I now send you shall be made an hundred.

It is gone so far, that the Marriage-Articles are ordered to be drawn up; and a Week's Time compleats my Misery; if you have not Skill, or good Nature enough, to prevent it, set your *Genius* to work then, I beseech you, and let me have an immediate Answer, if you have any Regard for the everlasting Repose of your Well-wisher, or would make a fast Friend of,

Your humble Servant.

P. S. Fold your Letter in the Manner I have done this, that nothing of what you write may be discovered by the Messenger.

LETTER VII.

From the same.

Mr. CAMPBEL,

I HAVE taken your Advice, and revealed the whole Matter to my Son, but with what Confusion on my Side, and Surprize on his, is easy to imagine: He, notwithstanding, behaved as he ought to do in the Affair, paid me the Duty owing to her that gave him Birth, and promised eternal Secrecy. Soon after he had taken Leave, a Letter came from him to my Spouse, excusing himself for not being able to accomplish his Contract, being, he said, obliged to leave *England* for many Years, if not for Life; and, I am told, he is now preparing in reality to Travel.

THUS am I eased of my most tormenting Dread, but am still in the utmost Sorrow; my poor Girl takes the imaginary Falshood of her Lover so much to Heart, that I question if she will be able to overcome it: I beg a little of your Assistance in this Affair also, and I shall never think I can enough repay your Goodness. I have heard something of your *Talismans*, if you imagine the wearing one of them will be of any Service to her, I desire you will enclose on in your Answer to this, or whatever else is in your Power for the Recovery of her Peace shall be

pur-

purchased at any Price, though I experienced the Generosity of your Temper too much to suspect you will exact, or, indeed, ask a sufficient Price from those you honour with your Friendship: leave the Payment therefore to myself, for I would act by Mr. *Campbel*, as he has done by me; continue only your Diligence and Secrecy, and depend on every Thing to serve you in the Power of,

Your infinitely obliged Friend.

LETTER VIII.

From a young Lady very much in Love.

SIR,

SO many of my Acquaintance having experienced your Skill in telling their Names at first Sight, I think it altogether needless to give you that Trouble, and would much rather you should employ your Genius in doing something more really to my Advantage than satisfying a foolish Curiosity; and as what I require, I believe may be done as well without seeing me, as if I were present. I send this to inform you, I have for these three Months been passionately in Love with a certain Gentleman, who never made any Addresses of that Kind to me: I have made it my Business to dive into the Design of his Visits every where, and by all I can hear, judge he has a Heart wholly unengaged. I fancy, therefore, it would

would be no difficult Thing for you to prepare something for me to give him, that might inspire him with Inclinations conformable to mine: If you can do this, I assure you of twenty Guineas the Moment I perceive the least Alteration, to my Advantage, in his Behaviour.

The Bearer will give you two Guineas by way of Earnest, and you may communicate your Thoughts as freely to her, as to myself. I desire you will not trifle with me, but let me know at once what is to be done, for be assured, such a Conduct will oblige me to be as much your Friend, as the contrary would make me your Enemy, and that shall make me capable of being either, as you shall deserve from,

Your unknown humble Servant.

LETTER IX.

From a Politician.

SIR,

NOTWITHSTANDING the Civilities with which you treated me, and which demand my particular Acknowledgments; I cannot forbear letting you know how much I regret that too great Caution in your Behaviour to me. You, who see so much into the Dispositions of Mankind, could not be ignorant that whatever you had

had communicated to me would have been kept
secret. It would be ridiculous, in one of my Character, to become a Blab; and whatever Use I
had made of your Instructions, the World should
never have been sensible they came from you.

IF, therefore, by your Gift of *Second Sight*,
or any other Intelligence, you foreknow any
thing concerning the Fate of *Europe*, which the
Knowledge of would be an Advantage to those
entrusted with the Management of publick Affairs; I cannot find any Reason for concealing
it.

I GRANT what you say is Truth, *That Things
of this Nature are not proper to be spoken of*; but
this is in Regard only of the Vulgar, who, wanting Sense to comprehend the Mysteries of true
Policy, judge every Thing according as it appears to their shallow Capacities: Among such,
indeed, you cannot be too circumspect, but with
a Person, who is perfectly acquainted with the
Interests of most Courts of *Europe*, methinks
you should have no Reserve.

IN fine, to convince me you have in reality
that Esteem for me you profess, you must be
more free at our next Meeting, which, if you
can get loose from that Circle of fair Visitants,
with whom I know your House is almost perpetually filled, I should be glad that it be deferred no longer than To-morrow, about Seven

in

in the Evening, at the *King's-Arms* Tavern, *Pall-Mall*. Let me know if I may expect this Favour, by my Servant, and conclude me,

Your real Friend.

LETTER X.

From a young Nobleman.

Dear CAMPBEL,

I WRITE to you now without any Fear of being discovered: I may now pass an Evening with you, whenever you have Leisure or Inclination, without being condemned to the Necessity of a lying Excuse that I have been somewhere else: In a Word, the whole Secret is out. My Father suspecting there was something in my Cabinet I would conceal from his Knowledge, broke it open this Morning, and took out all your Letters and Papers that passed between us in Conversation: They contain, it seems, some Secrets in the Family, to which he knew even myself must be a Stranger; and this has given him so great, and, indeed, so just an Opinion, both of your Skill and Candour, that he resolves very soon to consult you himself on a material Affair. He told me, *He was so far from condemning an Intimacy with you, that he was glad I had contracted one with a Person so very extraordinary, and who was capable of giving me such good Advice.*

What you wrote concerning Lady *R*———, a little shocked him, and he ordered me to enquire more particularly into that Business, and to know of you, whether there was any Possibility of changing her Resolution or not. I desire, therefore, that you will consult your Familiar about it, and be as punctual as you can in it. I hope the Pleasure of seeing you some time this Week, when I expect you will have an Answer ready for me, who am,

Unfeignedly yours.

LETTER XI.

From a Gentleman to whom Mr. Campbel *had lent the Book of his Life, and Spy on the Conjurer.*

Dear SIR,

I RETURN your Books with Thanks: I assure you the Perusal of them has afforded all this Family a great deal of Pleasure; but I must beg Pardon both of *Justitia* and the Writer of your Life, when I say, that tho' there are many surprising Narratives contained in both, they are infinitely short of what Experience assures me is in your Power. And I am confident, if my Affair, and its Event, which is entirely owing to your Art, had reached the Inspection of these Authors, it would have occasioned a larger and more

more learned Treatise, concerning the Possibility of such Discernment in a humane Mind.

But I dare believe these will not be the last Volumes published on the Transactions of a Person who has so deservedly the Esteem and Admiration of the World; when I hear of any such Thing on Foot, I shall not scruple relating how greatly I am in the Number of the Obliged; till then, I beg you will accept the more private Acknowledgments of,

S I R,

Your very humble and devoted Servant.

LETTER XII.

From a new-married Lady.

S I R,

AS I consented to marry the Gentleman who is now my Husband, meerly on your advising me to do so, and the Warning you gave me of Mr. G——, I think it my Duty to inform you, that my Preservation from the worst Calamity that can befal a Woman, is wholly owing to your so generously exerting your Art in my Favour. I have this Moment heard from unquestionable Evidence, that that perfidious Wretch has been, not only as you said, under a strict Engagement, but also the lawful Husband of

another

another for more than two Years: But you were cautious not to stretch the Truth, and that happy Caution saved me; for had you suggested any Thing beyond my Belief, to his Prejudice, I should have looked on all the rest as Malice. It would have been difficult to have given Credit to his being actually married, because our Families have been so long acquainted, and not the least Suspicion of any such Thing in either of them; but without one could see into the Heart, like you, 'tis impossible to be assured who a Person loves, or has addressed, provided the Parties themselves keep it private.

I CONFESS, he was once very dear to me, and it was not without the extreamest Reluctance I tore myself from him; nothing but your Menaces could have made me do it: But I am now happy, and flatter myself, from your Predictions, that I shall continue so. May all, to whom your Advice has been of equal Benefit, be always ready to acknowledge the Obligation, and you will then have many assured Friends. I shall rejoice to hear of your Health, and shall take it as no inconsiderable Addition to your former Favours, that you continue a Correspondence with,

SIR,

Your most obliged Servant,

LETTER XIII.

From an Adept.

SIR,

AS I told you, I could do nothing without the Consent of my Brethren, I no sooner left you than I dispatched Letters to every one of them, and have their Consent to admit you, as soon as the Death of any one among us shall make Room for so extraordinary a Person. I have already told you our Number was limitted to Twelve, and therefore this is all that can be granted.

I CAN never sufficiently admire your great Proficiency in this the most abstruse and occult Science under Heaven, to have attained, without the Assistance of any Learning, those Secrets of Nature, which so many Thousands have cracked their Brains, and expended their whole Estates in Search of, more testifies you to hold Intelligence with the invisible World, than all the wonderful Things you have foretold; yet, at the same Time shews, that both you and them are under a certain Limitation; otherwise it would be as easy for you to have obtained the Whole as Part. I am satisfied, if ever you are among the Number of the *Adept,* it will seem surprising to you, that it was necessary you should be perfect in this grand Secret.

There needed no more to assure me how near you were to the Matter, than your just Ridicule of those Persons who pretend to be Masters of the *Philosopher's Stone*, yet, at the same Time, confess themselves ignorant of the *Quintessence*, whereas one cannot be had without the other; but this is a Truth which these Smatterers are entirely ignorant of, and I never found acknowledged by any Students in this Art but yourself.

The Transmutation of Metals is so trifling a Thing, that I am amazed any wise Man can value himself for it; yet this is what passes on the Vulgar for the *Philosopher's Stone*, and by this has many a wealthy Person reduced himself to Beggary; and what is to be more lamented, the pernicious Effects of studying, and pretending to this Science, have brought into Contempt, what the real Attainment of, renders Men a kind of Gods on Earth.

I shall trouble you no farther at this Time; but wishing our three reigning Influences, *Sol, Mars* and *Mercury*, may befriend your Inquisitions, and conclude myself,

Your very faithful, &c.

LET

LETTER XIV.

From a young Gentleman at Cambridge.

SIR,

MACHIAVELL tells us, *That to be Merciful to our Enemies, is being Cruel to ourselves*; but I have diffented from that great Politician, to follow a Maxim of a latter Date, and, inftead of revealing the monftrous Impofition put on my Mother by her unjuft Steward, have endeavoured to footh his rugged Nature by Flattery and Submiffions. I imagine this has done me confiderable Service; for my Mother, who acts nothing but by my Directions, has wrote much kinder to me than fhe was accuftomed, while I declared myfelf averfe to this Favourit, and has added Fifty Pounds a Year to my Allowance.

I AM told, however, by fome whofe Years intitle them to a greater Share of Penetration than myfelf, that this Reconciliation is but a Feint, to have the better Opportunity of ruining me at once; which makes me entreat the Favour of you, Sir, to confult that never-failing *Genius* of yours in this Point; and alfo, whether my Mother will always continue to be fo infatuated with his Artifices, to the Prejudice, not only of her Children, but her own Reputation alfo. I
wifh

wish to Heaven there were a Possibility of bringing her to your House; I am certain you would have the Power of convincing her of her Error; but as there is not, we must be content to work by such Means as are allowed us.

It is needless to make any Apologies to you, who read the Mind, for troubling you so often, and so seldom giving any Proof of my Gratitude: You know my Hands are tied, and, also, that whenever I get them loose, I have the Will to shew, in something more than bare Acknowledgments, the just Sense I have of your repeated Favours; and that I am,

Your infinitely obliged,

and humble Servant,

P. S. I beg an Answer with all possible Expedition, and directed as usual.

LETTER XV.

From a Gentleman of the Town.

SIR,

I AM told, you glory very much in the good Offices you do, in making up Breaches in Families, and reconciling Persons at Variance: I now desire a Proof of this Sweetness of Disposition, and, if I find it, shall return the Obligation.

My

My Wife, who is of a Temper inclined to Jealousy, has been told of some private Visits I made to a certain Lady, and resolves to consult you on the Truth of it. I confess myself guilty not only of this Charge, but many others of the like Nature, which, I have that Opinion of your Skill as to believe you can inform her of. My Request is, that you will be as silent with your Pen on this Head, as you are on all others with your Tongue: To confirm her Suspicions, much more to let her into Secrets which yet she has no Notion of, would cause an endless Quarrel between us, and serve to make her more unhappy; for tho' I resolve within myself never to wrong her in this Point again, yet I shall, should she get so much the upper Hand of me, as to be reduced to ask her Pardon, and put it in her Power, whenever she has the Vapours, to reproach me with Injustice. As you are a married Man yourself, and know how necessary it is to keep Women in that Subjection they were created for, I flatter myself, you will take this into Consideration, and prevent from being exposed, and made uneasy for Life,

Your real, tho' unknown, Admirer.

LET-

LETTER XVI.

From a Gentleman at Bombay.

SIR,

THIS brings you an Account that I have unfortunately loft that excellent *Talisman*, to which, under Heaven, I certainly owed my Relief from all those Calamities I laboured under at my firft Acquaintance with you, and to entreat you will prepare another, and send it by the firft Ship, for I look for nothing but Ill-luck while I am without one.

I also beg your Advice concerning my Son *John*, who is very defirous of going to Sea, and tells me, *He has been promised ftrange Things in a Dream, and that he is fure of being a great Man if he follows that Employment.* I own I am very averfe to parting with him; but if his Defire be really the Impulfe of a good Angel, I would not oppofe it: I depend on you, dear Sir, to fet me right in this Matter, and as you have fo wonderfully raifed the Father out of his Troubles, vouchfafe alfo to direct the Son. Capt. *Tho. E* ⸺, who brings this, will pay three Guineas for the *Talisman*, which I once more conjure you may be fent with all poffible Speed; My Wife gives her beft Refpects to you and yours; which, with both our Wifhes for your Health and Profperity, is all that offers at this Time, from, *SIR*,

Your moft humble Servant.

LETTER XVII.

From an old Lady married to a young Man.

SIR,

I AM ashamed to approach you after having run headlong into the Ruin your friendly Caution would have saved me from; yet have no other Hope or Dependance in this World but in your Advice; if you will be so good to give it after the Neglect my ill Stars compelled me to use it with.

But not to keep you in Suspence, in spite of all you told me, I was married to Mr. J———, the Twelfth of last Month; I wish to God it had rather been the last of my Life, that I might not have had Cause to curse my inconsiderate Folly: In short, he is not worth a Groat; but, on the contrary, Debts are every Day coming upon him. Great Part of my Substance is already gone, and I doubt not but the Whole will be exhausted in the Payment of them if some Care be not immediately taken to prevent it. But notwithstanding all this, he uses me in the most barbarous Manner that can be imagined: The severest Reflections on my Age are the least of his Brutality; the least Answer I make to his Reproaches provokes him to Blows, and, I make no doubt, but he would murther me, if not restrained by the Law.

I am satisfied it is in your Power to help me, if you still can think me worthy of the Favour. Exert your good Nature, and forget what is past, nothing shall more readily obey your Injunctions for the future, nor return them with more Gratitude. Accept of five Guineas from *Judith*, and write by her your Mind at full to,

Your impatient, and most unfortunate, Servant.

LETTER XVIII.

From a Person of Quality.

SIR,

As none are so wise but they may be sometimes in an Error, so none ought to think themselves too great to acknowledge it: The first Step towards Amendment, is to confess we have done amiss, and the Readiness with which I now ask Pardon for my Behaviour, will, I doubt not, convince you that I am satisfied it was a Fault, and shall no more repeat it.

The Things you told me seemed so incredible, or if true, so impossible to be known by a third Person, that I am in hope my Excuse was partly made in your Breast; but however you may have condemned me, my Crime has been more my Punishment than, I am confident, the Sweetness of your Temper would suffer you to wish.

In

In fine, I have found, to my Cost, every Tittle of your Predictions were not without Foundation; and, if having doubted your Skill, has not forfeited all Claim to the Benefit of it, entreat you would exert yourself once more in advising how to behave in these Emergencies,

Your real Convert.

P. S. I shall be at the Place you first saw me at, this Evening, if more material Affairs will permit me the Pleasure of your Company; but let me know by the Bearer.

AN APPENDIX,

By Way of

VINDICATION

OF

Mr. *Duncan Campbel*,

AGAINST

That groundless Aspersion cast upon him, *That he but pretended to be Deaf and Dumb.*

By a Friend of the Deceased.

AN APPENDIX
By Way of
VINDICATION
OF
Mr. Duncan Campbel.

IF it be justly accounted dishonourable to speak more of People than we know they deserve, it is likewise so, in some Measure, not to correct those that do. Many a Falsity has passed for current Truth, meerly for the Want of Contradiction; and to keep Silence at an ill Report, which we are convinced is without Foundation, is to become Partner in the Author's Guilt, and an Assistant in his Slander.

This Confideration has roufed me up to fay fomething in Defence of my old Friend Mr. *Campbel*, in Anfwer to a fcandalous Affertion which was of fome Prejudice to his Intereft while living, and fince his Death, has been revived again in Malice to his Remains; I mean concerning his being naturally *Deaf* and *Dumb*, a Misfortune which has been cruelly and falfly reprefented as an Impofition on the Publick.

But before we proceed to give any Proofs on how little Foundation this idle Story is built, let us confult our own Reafon, what Probability there is that a Man fhould Counterfeit the Want of two fuch ufeful and pleafing Faculties as Speaking and Hearing; and what Advantage could poffibly accrue to Mr. *Campbel* from fuch a Pretence.

Every-body knows that his Gift of *Divination*, or foretelling Events, was the Confequence of *Second Sight*, which Faculty, Numbers befides him have been poffeffed of without being *Deaf* and *Dumb*, as there are many whofe Misfortune it is to be the *latter*, without being Mafter in any Degree of the *former* : As *Second Sight* therefore has not the leaft Relation to being *Deaf* and *Dumb*, how could it, in the leaft, advance either the Profit or Reputation of Mr. *Campbel* to be accounted fo? for on the contrary, 'tis eafy to demonftrate that he, being deprived of Speech and Hearing, was

of

of Prejudice to both; to his Interest, by preventing those People who could not write, and were unwilling to communicate their Affairs to a third Person from coming to consult him; and to his Reputation, by taking from him the Power of displaying those fine Talents he was Master of to Advantage, and also by drawing on him many Affronts, and rendering him liable to the Ridicule of the unthinking Vulgar.

It was also a considerable Expence to him, as he was never able to go Abroad either on Business, or a Party on Pleasure, without taking a Person with him who understood Finger-Conversation, and served him in the Nature of an Interpreter, and was paid for it accordingly.

All this is, I think, sufficient to convince any reasonable Man, that there was little *Probability* Mr. *Campbel* should counterfeit being *Deaf* and *Dumb*; let us now reflect on the *Possibility* of his doing so, for so long a Space of Time, if in Case it had really been as much to his Advantage as we have shewn it to have been the contrary.

In the first Place, to be a Proficient in Hypocrisy requires a Length of Time, and great Experience: Now there are several Persons still living who remember, and knew Mr. *Campbel* at fourteen Years of Age, and that he was then *Deaf* and *Dumb*: Can it be supposed that in those tender Years he could have acquired Artifice enough

enough to carry on a Deception of that Nature? No, he was then, doubtless, as all Youth are, little capable of keeping a Secret, much less of inventing and supporting a Contrivance in such a Manner as should deceive the most penetrating Judgment. Besides, he was not only at that Time, but even to the Day of his Death, one of the most open and undesigning Men on Earth; but as we are now talking only of what is possible to be done, whenever those who so possitively affirm Mr. *Campbel* was an Impostor in this Point, can produce an Instance of any one Man, who for the Space of five and thirty Years (for so long has the Object of our present Discourse been known in this Kingdom) who has carried on the like Deception, in all Humours, and in all Circumstances, and we will then allow that 'tis possible Mr. *Campbel* might have been guilty of the Crime laid to his Charge. How natural is it for us in any Surprize of Grief, or Joy, or any other Passion, to betray the sudden Emotion of our Souls by bursting into some Exclamation? Who can be always on their Guard on such Occasions? and how much more difficult would it be, when the Brain is over-charged with the Vapours arising from strong Liquor, when Discretion is lulled asleep, and even Remembrance is no more, to continue in a Constraint, such as avoiding the Use of Speech must necessarily be? Every one who had the least Acquaintance with Mr. *Campbel* is very sensible that there were few Men more addicted to Passion, or that

more

more indulged themselves in the Pleasures of the Bottle; yet, whenever he was overcome by the Excess of either, was he ever heard to utter the least articulate Sound? No, none that ever knew him will aver it; and if under such Circumstances he could still retain that Command over himself, it must be looked upon as a much greater Prodigy than his being able to tell the Name of any Person at first Sight, writing the most private Affairs of those he never saw, curing of Witchcraft, or any of those Wonders of Art which rendered him so justly famous while living, and will preserve his Memory while the Curiosity of knowing future Events has any Existence in the Minds of Men.

Oh! but they say he did not observe this perpetual Silence: *That whenever he was alone he used to throw off all Constraint, and indulge himself in the Pleasure of hearing his own Accents.* And moreover, *That he has been heard by Passengers, whom he imagined neither knew nor observed him, frequently talking in the Street, and Park, to his little Girl, a Child of about seven or eight Years old.* The first of these fine Stories, methinks, carries a manifest Detection of itself, for if he accustomed himself to speak at all, the less able would he have been to forbear it, whenever any of the Circumstances we have mentioned provoked him to it, or to render him forgetful of himself; and could he have been guilty of the latter, it would have implied

plied him *Fool*, as well as *Knave*, which as yet I never heard any-body fufpect him for.

Some too, not content with giving him the Character of an *Impoftor*, add alfo that of *Coward*, by pretending, *That they had made him find the Ufe of his Tongue by the Help of a Cudgel*; but this is a Reflection too palpably grofs to merit any Anfwer, and has been detected by a thoufand Inftances in the Behaviour of Mr. *Campbel*, which are too well known not to render the Repetition fuperfluous.

Were it poffible to trace thefe abfurd Inventions to their Origin, I am apt to believe we fhould either find the Authors would retract what they have faid, or their Characters in the World to be fuch as none would be willing to depend on the Veracity of, fo far as to report what they had alledged.

But what, or whoever they were, the Matter is not much to our prefent Purpofe; for I think it paft all doubt, that none can impartially confider the Reafons laid down in this *Defence*, without being ready to agree, that there was not even a *Poffibility*, much lefs a *Probability*, that Mr. *Campbel* either could, or would have impofed on the World in the Manner his Enemies have fuggefted.

It is certainly true, that on a firſt Acquaintance with Mr. *Campbel*, there was ſome Things to be obſerved in him which might puzzle an ordinary Capacity, and render him liable to Suſpicion without any Mixture of Prejudice or Malice : I mean the prodigious Gueſs he frequently had at the Purport of any Converſation which paſſed in his Preſence ; his tuning a Violin, and playing on it with great Exactneſs ; and many Inſtances of the like Nature, in which one would imagine the Ear was the only Agent of Information ; but when we conſider how uſual it is for the Almighty Diſpoſer of Nature to make up in one Senſe, what he thinks fit to deprive us of in another, nothing of this will appear ſtrange : What Mr. *Campbel* wanted in the Organs of *Speech* and *Hearing*, was abundantly compenſated for in thoſe of his *Sight* and *Touch* ; by the *firſt*, joined with an uncommon Quickneſs of Apprehenſion, he certainly had a wonderful Comprehenſion of what was ſaid, if he fixed his Eyes on the Perſon who ſpoke, and obſerved the Motion of their Lips ; and by the *other* he could diſtinguiſh Sounds, as was evident by putting the Neck of the Violin between his Teeth, and holding it there till he ſcrewed the Pegs to what Pitch he thought fit : The ſame Method he likewiſe took to know when his Watch was down. There are Reaſons both *Chirurgical* and *Philoſophical* for the *feeling of Sounds*, as may be ſeen at large in ſeveral learned Treatiſes ; and common Experience

ence may inform us, that a *deaf* Person, when he sees an Instrument of Musick touched, will immediately clap the Drum of his Ear to one End of a Stick, and hold the other against a hollow Board, and this will enable him to beat Time with as just a Cadence, as if he had the Sense of Hearing in the utmost Perfection.

This was the Method Mr. *Campbel* took to bear his Part in the Tunes play'd between the Acts at the Playhouse, as most of the Actors at both Houses, to whom he was perfectly known, can testify; yet does not this in the least imply that he was not *Deaf*, for take away the Assistance of his Stick and Board, and he would have been wholly unmoved at the most exquisite Performance.

For Proof of this Assertion I shall give, out of the innumerable ones I could produce, but two Instances, which several Gentlemen of undoubted Credit, and now living, were Witnesses of, and are ready to attest.

The first happened about some five and twenty Years ago, at which Time, as well as before, Mr. *Campbel* was a great Frequenter of Mr. *Meers's* Fencing-School, as were several other Gentlemen, some of his Scholars then, and others who had learned before, but came to improve themselves under the Instructions of so excellent a Master in that Art. These Gentlemen formed themselves

into

into a Society, and had a Meeting once every Week, laying themselves, in Case of Failure, under the Forfeiture of so much Money, which being constantly collected, made an annual Feast, all the Members were present. It was at one of those little Merry-makings that Mr. *Stephen Barnes*, a Gentleman of a plentiful Estate, and has now a considerable Place in the *Cursitor's-Office*, resolved to make an Experiment on Mr. *Campbel*; and accordingly put a Pistol in his Pocket, which, when he saw him busily engaged in Finger-Conversation with some of the Company that understood that kind of Dialect, he step'd behind him and let off just at his Ear. I would now ask any one of those zealous Assertors of Mr. *Campbel*'s Hearing, whether they think it possible for him to have refrained Starting, or by some Emotion of Body or Countenance have betrayed his Surprize at so unexpected a Sound? I believe they would answer in the Negative, and if so, must allow this to be a sufficient Demonstration of his being *Deaf*, for the Accident made not the least Alteration in him, and he went on with his Discourse totally unconcerned and insensible of it.

The Second is much of the same Kind; Mr. *Charles Manners*, a Gentleman nearly related to the illustrious Family of the Dukes of *Rutland*, sent for him to a Tavern, and under the Pretence of asking his Advice, proposed a Question to him in Writing, on the most difficult and intricate

tricate Matter he could invent, and in the midſt of Mr. *Campbel*'s deepeſt Speculation for the Explanation of it, gave the Signal to a Set of Drums, whom he had placed at the Door for that Purpoſe, to beat a March all at once; himſelf keeping his Eyes intently fixed on Mr. *Campbel*'s Face, who ſtill continued writing as he was before, quite unmoved at what, could he have heard, muſt have occaſioned ſome Alteration in his Countenance, even tho' he had been never ſo accuſtomed to it.

WHATEVER Opinion theſe Gentlemen had before, concerning the Reality of Mr. *Campbel's* being *Deaf* and *Dumb*, they were now perfectly convinced of it, as were ſeveral others who made Experiments of the like Nature.

BUT if there might poſſibly be ſome Excuſe for thoſe who did not weigh the Unreaſonableneſs of it, for believing him guilty of this Impoſition, while he lived, but his Death has taken away all the Shadow of it; and it would be taking from the King of Terrors, all that is ſo juſtly aſcribed to him, to imagine his Approach would not have put a Period to a Deception of this Kind.

IF Mr. *Campbel* had been ſnatched ſuddenly away, it might indeed have left a more plauſible Ground for Suſpicion, but when he laboured under a Complication of Diſtempers, and thoſe which are accounted the ſevereſt Racks that Human

man Nature can fuſtain, for many Days, I may ſay Weeks, and had his whole Frame diſtorted with Agonies, ſuch as were expected would divide the Body from the Soul, long before that Separation happened, were thoſe Moments to be employed in Diſſimulation? Would not thoſe Pangs have forced from him the long-hid Secret, which if it had been of Uſe to him, could now be ſo no more? To complain is as much the Conſequence of any violent Pain, as breathing is of Life, and the greateſt Heroes that the World ever produced, have not been able to reſtrain their Cries in the Tortures of a Fit of the Stone or Stranguary, or Gout, or many other Calamities to which our frail Mortality is incedent. Was Mr. *Campbel* more than Man? Could he at once repel thoſe dreadful Ideas which the near Proſpect of dark Futurity brings with it, and all Senſibility of the moſt conſummate bodily Miſery, be unmoved at all he now endured, and the Apprehenſions of what he might endure? Let us dreſs him in all the Virtues or Vices, of the very beſt, or worſt of Men, and we ſhall find ſuch a Belief is equally inconſiſtent with Reaſon and Experience: The Saints and Martyrs have not paſſed their fiery Tryal without teſtifying ſome Senſe of preſent Pain; nor have the moſt harden'd Sinners, when ſtanding on the Brink of Eternity, been able to diſguiſe their Horrors of the Future.

THAT Mr. *Campbel*, in his Long-Sickneſs, was never heard to ſpeak, there might be many Teſtimonials

timonials given, were it a Cause that required it, both by those who attended and watched him, and those who made him frequent Visits, either out of Friendship or Curiosity, being, perhaps, not quite satisfied before, and naturally concluding that now was the Time to be convinced.

It is not, therefore, to those who were personally acquainted with him, that I offer these Considerations in his Vindication, not doubting but every unprejudiced Person, who had the same Opportunity, has made the same Use of it as I have done, to be assured that there was not the least Foundation for believing him not *Deaf* and *Dumb* in Reality. But it is those who only know him by Report, and consequently were liable to be swayed by the Opinion of such as pretended to give a Character of him, that I would entreat to weigh well the Reasons I have given both for the *Improbability* and *Impossibility* of his having imposed on the World in this Point; and if either they, or those who have inspired them with this Belief, can produce better for the Proof of their Assertion than I have done against it, I shall readily submit; but if otherwise, expect mine may take Place: Or if (which indeed is but a vain Supposition) our Arguments should seem of equal Force, and the impartial Examiner be divided in his Opinion, I would only recommend one Thing to his Consideration, which is, that both Christian and Moral Doctrine teaches us, that in a dubious Case we are to give our Judgment in the most favourable

Man-

Manner. Besides, Generosity and Humanity oblige us to treat the Absent and the Dead with the utmost Tenderness: Mr. *Campbel* is now no more, and it would be the most unnatural Cruelty to brand his Memory with an Imputation of what, while he lived, was, at the best, only an ill-natured Suspicion, and which his long Sickness and Death confirmed to be entirely groundless.

Having heard that the foregoing Memoirs, which I know to have been wrote by himself, were about to be printed, I could not forbear asking Leave to subjoin my Sentiments on this Head, being excited thereto meerly by that Love of Truth which every honest Man, and Christian ought to make the Standard of his Actions; and if in so doing, I have confuted the malicious and falacious Reasonings of those who were causelesly his Enemies, or set right the Opinions of those who gave Credit to such Informations, meerly thro' neglecting the Considerations I have now laid before them, my End will be entirely answered, and I shall think the little Time I have spent in these Pages, could not have been better employed.

FINIS.

www.ingramcontent.com/pod-product-compliance
Lightning Source LLC
Chambersburg PA
CBHW020228170426
43201CB00007B/357